ADVANCE PRAISE FOR THE BOOK

'Sincere, succinct, and real. Pawan Kumar Marella's "cheat sheet" presents not only a heartfelt account of his travails over a long and illustrious career but also offers exceptional career advice for future leaders. His formulas for success are relatable, his examples endearing, and his inimitable style of writing are both insightful and entertaining. A great read for any rookie, this is a book that even corporate veterans will enjoy!'

—Rohit Jawa
CEO and MD, Hindustan Unilever Limited

'Pawan has encapsulated years of insights into this guide for navigating the corporate world. This book is filled with pearls of wisdom, waiting for the reader to collect them.'

—Geetika Mehta
Managing Director, Nivea India

'Through vivid storytelling and sharp insights, this book delivers the mentorship I wish I had when I started my career. An essential read for anyone wanting to make an impact early on.'

—Sunny Jain
Former Worldwide President of Beauty and Personal Care, Unilever

'An honest, insightful, and often humorous look at corporate life. Pawan's journey from rookie to leader is both inspiring and instructive.'

—Leena Chatterjee
Professor, BiTSoM, IIM Calcutta

'As I grew older, I found that my memory of the dilemmas young people face in their careers was dimming. Pawan has attempted to address those dilemmas with some sound, commonsense experiences.'

—R. Gopalakrishnan
Author and Corporate Advisor

'Equal parts wisdom and a wake-up call, Pawan's book dismantles the myths of corporate life and rebuilds them with unfiltered truths, all served with a healthy dose of humour and grit.'

—Shekar Khosla
Vice President Marketing, Google India

'In a world filled with jargon, acronyms, and contrived language, this book is a breath of fresh air. Its simple and practical wisdom, borne out of Pawan's many years of hands-on experience, makes it a must-read.'

—Prabha Narasimhan
Managing Director, Colgate Palmolive India

'Honest, insightful, and highly impactful. Written with humour, it's like having a seasoned mentor on demand. I wish I had this three decades ago when I was starting my corporate journey. The non-negotiables in particular, are spot on!'

—Manish Tiwary
Director of Special Projects, Nestlé

'Simple, practical, and real—this book answers questions you won't even think to ask until ten years into your career (by which time, it may be too late). I am making this mandatory reading for all first-time jobbers at The Whole Truth.'

—**Shashank Mehta**
Founder and CEO, The Whole Truth Foods

'A hands-on primer on how to navigate your career in a large organisation from short-term, mid-term, and long-term perspectives.'

—**Karthik Srinivasan**
Communications Consultant

'An honest, insightful, and often humorous take on corporate life. Having witnessed Pawan's journey up close, I can vouch that this book offers not just a blueprint for survival but also a guide to success.'

—**Kedar Lele**
Managing Director, Castrol India Ltd

'I was about to decline Pawan's request when the Wonka quote caught my eye and compelled me to read on. It's as useful for a rookie as it is for a fading general.'

—**Sudhir Sitapati**
Managing Director and CEO, Godrej Consumer Products

DEAR ROOKIE, DON'T PANIC

Your Cheat Sheet for Thriving at Work

PAWAN KUMAR MARELLA

HAY HOUSE INDIA
New Delhi • London • Sydney
Carlsbad, California • New York City

Hay House Publishers (India) Pvt Ltd
Muskaan Complex, Plot No. 3, B-2, Vasant Kunj, New Delhi – 110070, India

Hay House LLC, P.O. Box 5100, Carlsbad, CA 92018-5100, USA
Hay House UK Ltd, 1st Floor, Crawford Corner, 91-93 Baker Street, London W1U 6QQ, UK
Hay House Australia Publishing Pty Ltd, 18/36 Ralph St., Alexandria NSW 2015, Australia

Email: contact@hayhouse.co.in
Website: www.hayhouse.co.in

Copyright © Pawan Kumar Marella 2025

The views and opinions expressed in this book are the author's own and the facts are as reported by him. They have been verified to the extent possible, and the publishers are not in any way liable for the same.

All rights reserved. No part of this publication may be reproduced, by any mechanical, photographic, or electronic process, or in the form of a phonographic recording, nor may it be stored in a retrieval system, transmitted, or otherwise be copied for public or private use – other than for 'fair use' as brief quotations embodied in articles and reviews – without prior written permission of the publisher.

The author of this book does not dispense medical advice or prescribe the use of any technique as a form of treatment for physical, emotional, or medical problems without the advice of a physician, either directly or indirectly. The intent of the author is only to offer information of a general nature to help you in your quest for emotional, physical, and spiritual well-being. In the event you use any of the information in this book for yourself, the author and the publisher assume no responsibility for your actions.

First published by Hay House India, 2025
10 9 8 7 6 5 4 3 2 1

ISBN 978-93-66112-38-1
ISBN 978-93-66117-45-4 (E-Book)

DEDICATION

'It's not the chocolate that matters. It's the people you share it with.'
—Wonka's mother, *Wonka*

What you need to start is . . .
Not a mentor.
Not a buddy.
Not a coach.
Not a reminder.
Not a resolution.
Someone who can push you off the cliff of inertia.
Someone who can kick your behind to get off the chair of laziness.
Someone who gives a damn about your excuses and yanks the blanket off your cosy comfort zone.
Someone who really cares enough to throw you into the deep end.
Go find that someone.
This book is dedicated to my someone, my wife, Ruchi Agrawal Marella. Without her, I would be nowhere; with her, I can go anywhere.

CONTENTS

Foreword	11
Introduction	15
The Non-Negotiables	19

Part I: You Versus You

1.	Earning Your Stripes: A Rookie's Guide	27
2.	The Art of Being Effective and Efficient	43
3.	Navigating Competence, Choices, and Circumstances	59
4.	Crafting Your Personal Brand	73

Part II: You and Others

5.	Mastering the Art of Self-expression	93
6.	The Power of Asking the Right Questions	105
7.	The Secret to Successful Teamwork	123
8.	Navigating the Workplace Culture	139

Part III: The Future You

9.	A Guide to Getting Promoted	159
10.	First-time Boss: What to Expect	173
11.	Unlocking Your Leadership Potential	191
12.	Reflections: At the End of the Day	205

Frameworks	219
Epilogue: What Truly Matters	225
Endnotes	227
Acknowledgements	231

FOREWORD

As I pen this foreword, I am filled with excitement to introduce a book that's far more than just another corporate guide—it's a personal roadmap to thriving in the business world. Drawing from over two decades of experience across countries and cultures, Pawan offers a treasure trove of real-world lessons you won't find in any textbook.

What sets this book apart is its authenticity. Pawan doesn't just tell you what to do; he shows you through personal anecdotes, sharing moments of triumph as well as vulnerability. From navigating office politics to building your personal brand, each chapter is packed with actionable insights you can apply immediately.

Part I of the book, 'You Versus You', provides a vital framework for personal development in the corporate world. It emphasises the importance of self-awareness and understanding your unique strengths and values—qualities I believe are fundamental to authentic leadership. As I often say, 'If you can liberate yourself from self-limiting beliefs, you can unlock the incredible potential within you.'

Part II, 'You and Others', focuses on the essentials of working in a team, covering key aspects such as decision-making, team building, and communication. It aligns with my conviction that great leaders must cultivate a high moral quotient (MQ) alongside emotional intelligence (EQ) and intellectual capacity (IQ). What's particularly compelling about this section is its grounding in real-life scenarios. Pawan candidly discusses the challenges of leadership, sharing both successes and failures from his journey. This honesty offers readers a realistic perspective on fostering trust within teams and creating an environment where individuals feel empowered to innovate.

Part III, 'The Future You', addresses the crucial journey of becoming a leader. This section resonates deeply with my belief that the best way to lead is by being true to yourself. What impresses me most here is Pawan's ability to translate complex organisational theories into practical, implementable strategies. Through a series of personal experiences, the book demonstrates how leaders can build a culture of empowerment and collaboration.

What I appreciate most about this book is its practicality. It doesn't dwell on abstract theories; instead, it offers real strategies that work in the real world. Whether you are just starting your career or looking to take it to the next level, you will find invaluable advice on every page. As you read, you will feel like you have a mentor by your side, guiding you through the complexities of corporate life. Pawan's passion for empowering others shines throughout, making this an engaging and inspiring read.

In a world where career advice often feels generic or outdated, this book stands out as a must-read for anyone serious about making their mark in the corporate world. It's more than just a book—it's an investment in your future. So, turn the page and let your journey begin. Trust me, you won't regret it.

Happy reading, and here's to your success!

—**Nitin Paranjpe**
Chairman, Hindustan Unilever Limited

INTRODUCTION

'All we have to decide is what to do with the time that is given to us.'
— **Gandalf,** *The Lord of the Rings*

Le's kick off with a quick tour of my professional escapades. Think of it as a 'behind-the-scenes' to where all my insights in this book stem from. A little heads-up: my journey's as unique and worthwhile as anyone else's, peppered with biases and blind spots, just like yours.

1. **The Starting Block (Age 25)**

   Picture this—a late bloomer finally strides into the corporate world. My path was anything but straight. A year repeated in primary school, a university switcheroo across disciplines, a master's degree, and then landing a job in a field I hadn't formally studied! It was like fitting a square peg in a round hole, but somehow, it worked.

2. **The Decade of Discovery (Age 25-35)**

   Fast-forward through five cities across India, each move a new chapter. Here, life tossed me two of its best gifts: convincing my now-wife to marry me and welcoming our first son. This era was a cocktail of self-doubt, career highs and lows, and a constant battle between loving and loathing my job. From exhilarating escapades (think unintentional newspaper fame and adrenaline-pumped misadventures) to soul-searching, this phase was the inspiration for the You Versus You section.

3. **The African Adventure (Age 35-42)**

   Then came Ethiopia—thirteen months of literal and figurative sunshine. Starting from scratch in a land unknown, it was about taking risks and building anew. Here, my past expertise was just a starting point. I had to earn trust and create my niche all over again. After three years of in-house start-up hustle and the drama-filled birth of my second son, Nairobi beckoned with its lush landscapes and multifaceted challenges. Africa taught me humility, the art of unlearning, and a newfound respect for its people and culture. It's here that I found my true purpose, shaping much of the You and Others narrative.

4. **The Global Perspective (Age 42 to Present)**
   Fast forward to my current global role at headquarters, where the game changed from frontline operations to strategic long-term thinking. Collaborating across departments, I learnt to balance immediate goals with future planning, educate myself on the art of senior stakeholder management, and understand how difficult it's to take strategic decisions. This chapter of my journey is the crux of The Future You section, where past experiences blend into a more holistic professional outlook.

So, buckle up! What follows in this book is a collection of insights drawn from these diverse chapters of my life, each with its unique flavour of lessons and learnings.

THE NON-NEGOTIABLES

*'It's not who I am underneath,
but what I do that defines me.'*
— Batman, *Batman Begins*

Ever feel like you are drowning in a sea of career advice? Like you are trying to build a skyscraper without a blueprint? Let's face it, the corporate world can be a jungle, and sometimes it feels like we are all just winging it. In my experience, the foundation of everything we will talk about rests on four foundational non-negotiable pillars highlighted below. And if you take away only one thing from this book, let it be these!

1. **Health: Never Forego, Never Forget**

   Remember those days when you felt invincible? The long work hours, the strange eating habits, the binge-watching, jumpy sleep patterns—everything seems doable. It's like a new phone battery that's full and slowly ticking down without you realising till it's at five per cent one fine day and then you scramble for a charger. The only thing with your life is that the longer you wait to recharge, the more difficult it's to recharge to 100 per cent. Focusing on your holistic health and well-being from the start is the foundation for everything. Physical health (exercising regularly), mental health (taking breaks), emotional health (cultivating relationships), and purposeful health (finding your why). These are the four elements to invest in to survive and thrive. And at the end of the day, realising that health is everything, and nothing in the corporate world is worth sacrificing your health for, is probably the biggest non-negotiable of them all. If there's one lesson I would love for you to remember at the end of the book, it's this: your health is non-negotiable. It matters to you and to those who care about you. It's your superpower. Protect it, prioritise it, and never take it for granted.

2. **Integrity: No Shades of Grey**

   In the real world, the difference between right and wrong is not as simple and clear as we might assume. The line between bending and breaking a rule is hazy and assuming that if everyone is doing it, it must be okay is also not true. So, what do you do? Developing your own moral compass and setting personal principles is invaluable. Understanding the rule of law and the policies of your organisation is equally important. And never underestimate the timeless lessons of decency and respect instilled by your kindergarten teacher—they should continue to guide us even as adults. Integrity isn't just about following rules; it's about staying true to yourself and others. It forms the foundation of trust, respect, and long-term success. Always remember that integrity is integral!

3. **Trust: The Connecting Thread**

   Imagine trust as the invisible electricity that powers every relationship, every team, every dream. What if I told you that this single, intangible force could be the difference between a career that merely exists and one that truly thrives? In the complex landscape of professional success, trust is the hidden currency—more valuable than skills and more powerful than talent. It stems from your intent and impact, serving as the invisible thread that weaves individuals into high-performing teams. Trust is evident in everything, from the simple act of delivering on your promises (like sending a report by 5 p.m. when you said you would) to the larger act of sharing credit for success. Nearly everything you rely on others for in life depends on trust. Simply put, trust is a must!

4. **Showing Up: The Power of Compounding**

   From the time we were kids, attendance was always considered important—schools would make a big deal if you missed even one day. Then, as you grow up, you just get yourself to work, in person or virtually, almost like a natural conditioning from the school years. But what differentiates those who succeed and do well, in my experience and observation, are those who truly show up—mind, body, and soul—day after day, come what may. The ability to stay in the present, focus on your work and your meetings, read the pre-reads, not slack, and train your mind to get things done again and again is what makes the difference. You can almost tell who will succeed and make an impact by checking this one thing in people. Train yourself to show up. Have someone kick your butt or build routines and get tools to help—do what it takes but show up. It will compound, and you will thank your younger self for it later in life. So, show up to move up!

Health, integrity, trust, and showing up (HITS) have been the foundation of my success and resilience. As we explore further, remember that these core values will serve as a compass, guiding you on your journey to success.

Part I
You Versus You

'It is our choices, Harry, that show what we truly are, far more than our abilities.'
— Albus Dumbledore,
Harry Potter and the Chamber of Secrets

Not so long ago, I woke up one morning struggling to breathe. I found myself gulping for air as I got up and started pacing around. A few deep breaths later, I felt okay. Then on my way to the office and again on the way back, the same feeling returned—like I wasn't getting enough air in my lungs. I began taking deep breaths, gulping in air through my mouth and nose. After a few minutes, I felt better. This pattern repeated for a few days, prompting me to visit the company doctor, who promptly referred me to the best specialists in town.

A few days, multiple tests, pricks, and probes later, I sat across from a bemused doctor who handed me a piece of paper, saying, 'Here's your prescription, Pawan.' Relieved, I glanced at it, only to find it blank. Flipping it over, still blank, I looked up at the doctor with a puzzled expression. He said, 'Young man, you have forgotten how to breathe. There's nothing physically wrong with you. All your tests are normal. You have simply forgotten to breathe, possibly due to stress.' At once, I felt both relieved and stressed—stressed that I was stressed and didn't even know it!

Long story short, taking a step back and gaining perspective on my work, its impact on me, my team, my family, and the world around me made me realise how much I needed to change—starting with how I dealt with myself. This eye-opening experience highlighted how easy it is to lose touch with ourselves in the fast-paced corporate world. It's not just about forgetting to breathe; it's about losing sight of who we are, what truly matters, and how to navigate our careers effectively.

As I reflected on this incident and my journey so far, I identified four key areas essential for thriving in a career while staying true to oneself. These insights form the foundation of this section, You Versus You, where we will explore the internal battles we face and how to overcome them.

1. **Earning Your Stripes: A Rookie's Guide**

   These are reflections on what I wish I had known when I was a newbie trying to earn my stripes. Some people are more prepared than others when the race starts. In hindsight, I would say I was less prepared than most, which meant I had to learn a lot along the way—often the hard way!

2. **The Art of Being Effective and Efficient**

   This section focuses on mastering the art of being both efficient and effective. It's not just about getting things done but ensuring you are doing the 'right' things, even amidst the noise and chaos that often surrounds us at work. It offers practical insights into staying grounded and achieving results in a realistic, sustainable way.

3. **Navigating Competence, Choices, and Circumstances**

   Next, I delve into navigating competence, choices, and consequences, discussing how to hone your skills, make smart decisions, and acknowledge the often-underestimated role of luck in shaping your journey.

4. **Crafting Your Personal Brand**

   Finally, this part wraps up with a focus on crafting your personal brand—an essential yet underrated skill that's rarely taught but crucial for standing out and making a lasting impact.

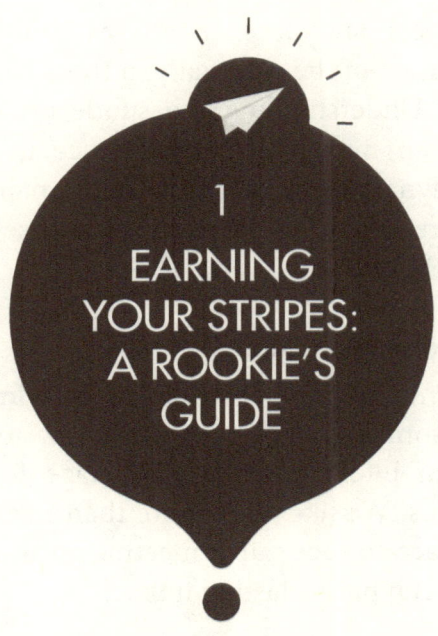

1
EARNING YOUR STRIPES: A ROOKIE'S GUIDE

Hello, Is There Anybody Out There?

Hey there! Ever wonder why sometimes things at work just . . . stall? Here's a little brainteaser for you: Remember the one person you didn't greet during your first 100 days at work? Turns out, they might be the very same person jamming the gears on your current project. Surprised? Let's dive a bit deeper.

From what I have seen, the secret sauce for smooth sailing at work isn't just about agreeing on everything or being best buddies—it's about trust. And guess what? Trust doesn't just magically appear. It starts with something as simple as a 'hello' and a handshake.

In the early days of a new job, taking the time for a no-strings-attached meet-and-greet does wonders. Why?

It shows respect and appreciation as well as a genuine acknowledgement of the fact that you think the other person is important. Understanding the subtle art of connecting with others can make all the difference in personal and professional dynamics. Let's look at how small yet impactful actions can create lasting connections and set the stage for meaningful relationships.

1. **First Impressions Count**

    Like it or not, we are hardwired to form snap judgments. Meeting someone early on puts a face to a name, and that initial interaction sets the stage for your future interactions. We like faces more than names, so making that first face-to-face call or meeting meaningful from the very start can have a lasting impact.

2. **Finding Common Ground**

    When we first meet someone, our brains act like little detectives, instinctively searching for common ground. Maybe it's having kids the same age or cheering for the same sports team. These shared interests create a subtle sense of belonging to the same group and help later when it comes to working on shared goals as a team. Building these connections early lays the groundwork for collaboration and trust, making teamwork smoother and more productive in the long run.

3. **The Power of Unplanned Connections**

    Meeting someone without immediately needing something from them leaves a lasting impression. It's like an unspoken rule of reciprocity: You took the time for me; I owe you one. And sometimes, it's refreshing for the other person to have a call where no decisions need to be made, and no views need to be shared. Such an approach fosters goodwill and strengthens relationships, making future interactions more genuine and meaningful.

I have seen the wonders of making these early connections and the pitfalls of skipping them. It took me many years, but I finally got the hang of it in my current role, where I was completely dependent on people who did not report to me to get work done. Perhaps that realisation made the difference, and I am thankful for it. I spent my first 100 days speaking to over 200 people, both closely and distantly connected to my work. And what wonders it did. People remembered that I had reached out early on when it was time to work. They remembered that I had asked, 'How can I help?' rather than asking for help at the start. Take it from me: trying to build this bridge when you are 300 days into your job will be like trying to start a diet on Diwali—awkward and kind of too late.

The one person you missed saying hello to in your first 100 days is the same person holding up your work today!

Rookies: Ready to Earn Your Stripes?

Stepping into the corporate world for the first time can feel like being thrown into a game where everyone knows the rules—except you. But here's the good news: you have got this. Let's talk about some insider tips to help you not just survive but thrive in your new role. These come from my own experiences as a rookie in every new stint I have taken on, as well as from training many newcomers along the way.

1. **Hard Work Now, Smart Work Later**

   This is the time for relentless hard work. Forget the trendy work-life balance mantra for now. Your first year is where you are mentally primed to learn the most. Put in the effort, and you will find more people eager to teach you and bring you into the fold. Like it or not, your boss is looking to see if you are putting in the effort, as they did the same.

2. **Don't Just Fit In, Stand Out**

   When it comes to accepting things as they are, that's where you don't want to fit in. These are times of rapid change, and organisations need to adapt continually. Fresh ideas often come from new minds. If you have questions and better thoughts, share them. You might be the fresh perspective your company needs.

3. **Fit in with Values**

   If your personal values clash with your company's, it might be a sign to move on. However, if there's alignment, embrace the company values. They will guide you in tricky situations, helping you make the right decisions, irrespective of peer pressure.

4. **Craft Your Success Story**

   Everyone loves a good success story. Find one problem, big or small, fix it, and make that your claim to fame. Your confidence will soar, and a compelling story will always put you in the 'in' crowd. Ask for more work beyond your comfort zone so that even if you don't fully succeed, your boss sees you stretching.

5. **Get Your Boss on Your Side**

It is important to gain your boss's support, not by being subservient or a 'yes' person, but because you will need their backing when you begin making significant decisions and challenging established norms. Their support is crucial, especially given your relative inexperience. Once that's in place, you are officially 'in'!

My first stint as an area sales manager was a rollercoaster of mishaps and missteps. I fell into the trap of trying too hard to impress, attempting to juggle too many tasks instead of focusing on the essentials, and failing to garner support from my boss. At the six-month mark, a fortunate organisational reshuffle placed me in a new role, accompanied by a candid wake-up call from my boss. I can still recall the scene vividly—sitting in the company guest house, sipping lukewarm tea as my boss delivered the unvarnished truth. It was a pivotal moment that taught me that true kindness involves offering honest feedback. I also remember feeling that the tea tasted just as I felt—lukewarm! Anyway, it was a wake-up call. If you are a newbie, I would urge you to ask for regular feedback. Most folks would have an annual or bi-annual feedback cycle but as a newbie, that's just too late. If you can get a rhythm of feedback much more regularly, it will benefit you. And you asking for it itself makes a big positive impression.

Back to my story. After receiving that feedback, a mix of inherent competitiveness, fear, anger, and desperation drove me to change course. I focused on showing up every day and working harder than anyone else. I thought differently, tackled one big thing at a time, stayed true to my values, and got my boss on my side through regular updates and advice sessions. This was combined with consistent feedback—not just from my boss, but also from the team I managed. I clarified expectations, understood what would be valuable, and made that my mantra for the team.

The team I managed was the smallest by turnover in the region, and to make an impact, we had to grow the fastest and position ourselves as the place where people could come to earn their stripes—an underdog story, if you will. And it worked! That underdog mentality fuelled me and the team with an energy and passion that was unmatched. I never again underestimated the power of making people feel they are part of something important, something bigger than themselves, where they feel valued, respected, and appreciated. My team performed well, the results were outstanding, I thrived, many of those I managed were promoted, and here I am, years later, reflecting on the journey. Overall, the key takeaway from this entire story is that as a newbie, earning your stripes demands nothing less than relentless hard work and unwavering commitment. In other words, if you want it, you must put in the effort.

The first job formula: Go all-in + Challenge the norms + Live your values + Design for success + Partner with your boss.

Do First, Talk Later

If you are new to a role and a team, rather than talking a lot about your intent, it's better to deliver a strong initial impact.

The output builds the foundation of trust that you can get stuff done. Then folks around you will listen when you say something. On the other hand, if you have been around for a while in a role and with a team, your intent matters more. Now that you have been through it all, what you truly believe in, what you want to achieve next, and why others should join you in that mission become even more important. Remember, impact builds trust in the short term, while intent builds trust in the long term.

I used to wonder why no one wanted to listen to me when I first started working; now, I know. I was being tested on my ability to get things done, not my debating and talking skills. I was being told to let me work to do the talking. Let me share a story that highlights this.

I started as a distributor salesperson, responsible for visiting various mom-and-pop stores and collecting orders for products to be serviced the next day. It sounded easy at first, but boy, did I learn the hard way. I was a mix of anxiety and excitement, insecurity and stimulation—sweaty palms, nerves running high! It turns out that store owners are incredibly busy, and learning the art of crafting the perfect elevator pitch for new products is much tougher than I thought. Eventually, I realised that showing them the product and leaving a sample with them worked best. Asking for payments owed to the distributor was another tricky part. My salary was always deposited at the end of the month, and I never had to ask my boss for money! I learnt that it's best to ask for payments professionally at the start of the conversation and stick to the rules set at the beginning—kind of like tackling the toughest part of the day first. This became a life lesson for many things later.

Food was another challenge. I learnt the importance of eating healthy at home—a solid breakfast, a proper dinner, and sacrificing lunch for fruits to stay healthy. I also learnt the subtle art of negotiation and the balance of power. The store owners could sense when I was desperate for a sale and would try to negotiate for better deals. So, working smart to maximise opportunities when a good deal came my way and not squandering them became another valuable lesson. I also gained firsthand insight into what consumers really think about your products. There's no need for market research agencies when customers tell you the issues directly, day in and day out. Patterns emerge, and the realities become clear. I also learnt the importance of safety. Spending so much time on the road, I made it a non-negotiable rule to wear helmets on a bike and seatbelts in a car.

I have learnt so much more, but these are just a few glimpses of the value of experiencing things firsthand. Being on the front lines, rolling up your sleeves, and doing the actual work yourself calms your nerves, opens your mind, builds knowledge, and boosts confidence, self-respect, and self-worth. And that makes all the difference. Try it!

No do means no talk—just listen.

Playing Football or Tennis?

It may not be immediately clear why I have asked this question or what I mean by it. Let me explain.

In football, success depends on teamwork and collaboration. In contrast, in tennis (singles), your individual skill is what matters most. The same principle applies to careers. If you choose to be a financial analyst, your individual skills and expertise are crucial to your success. However, if you choose to work in a field like consumer packaged goods (CPG), your ability to collaborate and work effectively with others is the key to success.

So, if you work in a sector or company where collective effort is essential, stop complaining about how hard you are working while others aren't pulling their weight. The key skill you need to develop is how to work with others—how to influence, motivate, and get things done together. Once you understand this, your role and the expectations of the organisation will become much clearer.

Two books that taught me many practical tips on this subject are *How to Win Friends and Influence People* by Dale Carnegie (yes, that very old book!) and *Influence: The Psychology of Persuasion* by Robert B. Cialdini, PhD.

Do not come to a football match and play tennis.

To Break the Rules or Not?

We have all heard the saying: 'Break all the rules.' It's a phrase that has become common in many areas of life, from business and entrepreneurship to the arts. My perspective on this is simple: to break the rules, you first need to know and understand them.

The reality is that we live in a VUCA (volatile, uncertain, complex, and ambiguous) world. The pressure to act quickly, to shift tactics mid-project, and to abandon something and start something new has become the norm. But how do you navigate this fast-paced environment, changing decades of established methods and speeding through traffic jams created by systems and processes designed to keep things in check? The answer, whether simple or complex, is the same: know the rules first. This means that you need to understand how things were done and why, so you can figure out what can be bypassed and how to do it. You need to distinguish between the must-haves and the nice-to-haves, and recognise the risks involved when breaking the rules, so you can take appropriate steps to mitigate them. Understanding how things work now is essential if you want to change them for the better. It's like being asked to untangle a complicated sailor's knot in record time. If you don't know how the knot was tied in the first place, it's going to be nearly impossible to unravel it quickly. So, first, learn the rules, then break them.

To innovate and create change, first understand the existing rules before you challenge them.

Nurture Your Relationships

In today's chaotic world, there's a growing craving for certainty and a sense of belonging. As the corporate scene mirrors this chaos, we find ourselves huddling closer to our inner circles, seeking that reassuring 'it's okay'. Therefore, it's important to have a close-knit, accessible support system. It's this inner circle that keeps us grounded and resilient, more so than relying on strangers, aid organisations, or even the government.

Don't hesitate to ask for help. Call your family. Stay in touch with friends from school and college. They know you best and will tell you the truth. When things are not going your way, they will remind you of your strengths and how good you are and when things are going well, they will keep you grounded and not treat you like a superstar and won't boost your ego even higher! Also, make time to make new friends. Go out to office parties, eat in the canteen with someone, hover at the water cooler a bit longer, and seek virtual coffee catchups. And then, be the shoulder someone leans on. Pass it on. Be there for someone like they were there for you.

The natural cure to chaos = Nurturing your relationships.

Don't Be Shy to Extend an Invite

Ever find yourself so absorbed in your work, your project, or your task that you completely lose sight of the bigger picture? It's like the classic saying about missing the forest for the trees. On such occasions, a handy piece of advice is to invite someone to look at what you are working on. Someone not immersed in your project can provide a fresh perspective. They might help you see the bigger picture you have been overlooking, point out obvious details you have missed, and even surprise you by highlighting what you are doing exceptionally well.

If you have built and nurtured your relationships from the start, you will have plenty of cheerleaders and supporters who will be happy to step in and help. I have seen time and again how inviting a fresh perspective leads to those aha moments much faster than wrestling with a mental block all alone. Sometimes, all it takes is an outside view to reignite clarity and creativity.

Invite someone over to offer a fresh perspective.

Write Your End-of-Year Appraisal Note on Day One

What a ludicrous piece of advice, right? Suggesting you write your end-of-year appraisal on the very first day of your job—have I gone mad? Not at all. Over time, I have realised the importance of starting with the end in mind. This concept is beautifully articulated in Stephen R. Covey's *The 7 Habits of Highly Effective People*, where his second habit is: Begin with the end in mind.

Picture this: it's appraisal time, and your boss asks you to review the year and share your key achievements. If you are anything like me, you might scramble to recall results, only to realise you overlooked certain areas or lacked impactful stories to share. It's a situation I know many can relate to.

The turning point for me came when I began drafting my appraisal at the start of the year. I imagined what a stellar appraisal would look like and then aligned this vision with my boss. This process took effort and time, but the payoff was immense.

It's about taking charge of your destiny by imagining your success and working toward it deliberately. Give it a try! Here's an example of what I wrote for one of my roles on day one. It's edited for confidentiality but captures the essence:

1. I was a highly trusted and committed team member, earning trust both in terms of my intent and my competence (results).
2. I acted as an effective sparring partner and mirror for my boss and team members, facilitating better outcomes through a 'wisdom of crowds' approach.
3. I helped craft a fit-for-purpose strategy and ensured the team focused on turning strategy into actionable results, delivering on commitments.
4. I prioritised self-learning to improve my skills in new areas while staying true to my purpose as a leader and teacher by dedicating time regularly to learning and personal growth.
5. I built strong equity in the system through my performance, potential, newly acquired skills, sharpened old skills, diverse experiences, and living my purpose. As a result, I was regarded as a top talent and a highly valued resource for the organisation.

I shared this framework with my boss during every appraisal. We discussed my progress, which helped me stay focused on the big-picture outcomes I wanted from the role while tackling immediate monthly, quarterly, and yearly goals. In the end, investing time in dreaming about the end goal wasn't just helpful—it was transformative.

Envision your success early, align it with your goals, and work deliberately to achieve it.

Have Someone on Speed Dial

If you don't have anyone in your office you can chat with, you are either the CEO or in the wrong office! On a serious note, having someone to talk to without an agenda is essential. We all need that person we can gossip with, open to, and share our hopes and fears with, free from judgement.

If you are fortunate enough to have colleagues you can ping, talk to, or walk over to for a quick chat, that's great. But if you don't, it's worth reflecting on why that's the case. Is it something about the work environment? Or have you not made the effort to connect? Either way, it's important to reach out, even casually. Checking in with teammates just for a chat can work wonders—for them and for you.

I used to feel guilty about those quick trips to the tea stall when I worked in India. Over time, however, I realised just how much those breaks helped relieve stress. Now, I do something similar in a virtual setting by sending a simple, 'Hi, free for a chat?' message on the internal app. These small moments of connection make a big difference.

Build casual connections at work to foster trust, reduce stress, and strengthen team dynamics.

Key Takeaways

- The one person you missed saying hello to in your first 100 days is the same person holding up your work today!
- The first job formula: Go all-in + Challenge the norms + Live your values + Design for success + Partner with your boss.
- No do means no talk—just listen.
- Do not come to a football match and play tennis.
- To innovate and create change, first understand the existing rules before you challenge them.
- The natural cure to chaos = Nurturing your relationships.
- Invite someone over to offer a fresh perspective.
- Envision your success early, align it with your goals, and work deliberately to achieve it.
- Build casual connections at work to foster trust, reduce stress, and strengthen team dynamics.

2
THE ART OF BEING EFFECTIVE AND EFFICIENT

The Power of Sprints: Harnessing Focus and Efficiency in Your Work

It is vital to understand that work is not a steady-paced marathon. On the contrary, work often happens in sprints, which is why deadlines are so important. As the deadline approaches, the mind accelerates, pushing forward with renewed energy and focus. Have you ever felt that surge of energy when a deadline is looming? Our brain makes connections we didn't even know existed, all in the race to get things done.

If you are aiming to accomplish something effectively, set a deadline. Break your project into smaller steps, each with its own deadline, rather than one big, overwhelming deadline. This approach allows you to identify challenges early and address them as they arise. Of course, avoiding distractions is critical—otherwise, why bother?

My approach generally consists of creating dedicated slots of time for focused work in short bursts, or sprints, free from distractions. For example, I keep my phone away during these times. Finding the right time and energy to do your best work is crucial. For me, that's the afternoon, not early morning. Over time, I have structured my day so that meetings happen in the morning and my afternoons remain free. This simple change makes a huge difference. Even this book was written in focused sprints. First, I broke the larger idea into smaller sections and then, the focused sprints allowed me to stay sane by starting and finishing one section at a time. To make these sprints more effective and sustainable, I developed three key work habits that helped me stay on track:

1. **Weekend Time Blocks**

   I set aside specific time slots on weekends for writing, helping me build a routine and discipline. And I made sure to reward myself each time I hit a milestone; small celebrations helped keep me motivated.

2. **Idea Capture**

   I always had something nearby to jot down new ideas that came to me. This allowed me to expand on them later. Being prepared is half the battle.

3. **Family Understanding**

   I made sure my family understood that when I was 'in the zone', I needed uninterrupted time to focus. They knew to let me dive into my work without disturbances.

These three elements came together to help me complete this book in focused, efficient, and effective sprints. At least, that was the plan. But, as you can guess, it didn't always go exactly as planned. For example, I initially treated these sprints as a selfish affair, monopolising my time, which eventually required adjusting my sprint schedule to better accommodate everyone else around me. I learnt to resist the urge to jump up and start writing whenever inspiration struck, and instead, I started jotting down ideas for later expansion.

The big lesson? Work in sprints—but make it work for you, for those around you, and for the reality of the situation you are in.

Effective work happens in efficient sprints.

Right Moment to Focus Versus Focusing in the Moment

In most corporate jobs, almost every task is interdependent. It's rare to find a role where what you do doesn't impact others in the organisation. And while it's great to follow advice like 'find your zone', 'work based on your energy', and 'work in focused sprints', the reality is that you also need to develop the skill to get things done regardless of how you are feeling. Simply put, it's about building the muscle to power through tasks—even if it's a late Friday afternoon or an early Monday morning. Sometimes, you will need to work on a tedious task, like a zombie spreadsheet, when you would rather be brainstorming big ideas, all because of shifting deadlines or unexpected changes.

The truth is, work is what it is. When it's time to do it, you must get it done. And the key is learning how to focus in the moment you are in, instead of waiting for the 'perfect' moment to focus. Those who can do this—who can power through, no matter the circumstances—are the ones who succeed because they consistently get things done, come what may.

Sometimes, you must sprint when you are not up for it.

Last Minute Panic Is Okay

I seem to always find myself working to finish things at the last minute. As mentioned earlier, the real sprint often happens when deadlines approach. To ensure the quality of my work, I have found that setting multiple internal deadlines for different stages of a project might be more effective. It's like the last-minute panic, but in stages! This approach works particularly well when a project or task requires collaboration from multiple teams, especially considering the typical challenge of getting people together unless there's a fire to put out.

Having stage-wise deadlines allows you to track progress regularly and make timely adjustments—whether it's starting, stopping, or modifying aspects of the project—so you are not left scrambling at the last minute when it's too late to change course. Over time, I have also learnt to clear my desk of routine work as the final deadline approaches. There will inevitably be last-minute issues: the printer will malfunction, the latest version might not be saved, unexpected costs will pop up, or a calculation error will surface—basically, all the drama you would expect in a whodunit.

So, plan for the panic. Make room for the inevitable disruptions, and you will be better equipped to stay calm and solve problems as they arise.

Last-minute panic is okay—just make sure it happens in stages.

Switch Off and On

We have all heard the universal fix for 90 per cent of computer problems: 'Have you tried turning it off and on again?' This is true at work as well. If you are completely stuck on an issue, it might be a good idea to switch off and switch on again after a while.

In such cases, switching off would relate to mentally disconnecting. This could involve putting the task at hand in cold storage and forgetting about it for a while, or taking a real vacation, or doing anything that helps you take a complete break (switching off) from the issue and then coming back to start working on it again (switching on). The time off might just trigger different thoughts on how to tackle the issue, courtesy of multiple factors, such as the unconscious mind working on the matter and the brain being in an alpha state, which is more relaxed and leads to more innovative thoughts. And who knows? You might get the breakthrough you have been looking for.

I vividly recall the time when I was nearing the end of one of my stints and had to apply for other potential jobs through the internal job portal. It had been a while since I had begrudgingly updated my internal resume, so I updated it by looking at options online—the usual two-page Word document in black and white, listing what I had worked on, what I was responsible for, and the results—utterly uninspiring. I applied for roles, but nothing happened. Maybe I was fatigued, or maybe I was overconfident, but I realised something needed to be done. This was also around year-end (December), so we decided to take a family vacation. We went off the usual plan and rented a place on a beach in a small town. It was a very quiet place with no noise, no distractions, and no one around. It was like switching off from the busy world completely.

A few days in, walking on the beach, inspired by the tranquillity and uniqueness of that place, I thought to myself: my resume needs to stand out. It needs to look different, for starters, so that someone will stop, pick it up, and open it to read. It must be impactful in outlining why I am a good fit for the role and needs to make me interesting enough for someone to want to talk to me. I spent the next few days thinking and revised my resume into a PowerPoint deck, with sharp details of my work results, skills, photos, and visual examples of my work. I even added an entire section on my purpose and passions. And lo and behold, I went from no calls to multiple calls, with some very interesting people wanting to talk to me, all because I switched off. The profound benefits of seeking a serene and tranquil place to switch off are more powerful than we realise.

Believe in the power of taking a complete break.

Sudden Start, Sudden Stop

Every time we make our way to the office, we mentally gear up for work, get ready for the challenges, and outline the big things that need to get done that day. As we get closer to the office, we allow work to occupy more of our minds, like a warm-up before exercise. Similarly, when we head back home, we mentally prepare for home, leaving the office behind, knowing that tomorrow will be another day to take a crack at things. We think about what awaits us at home—people yearning for us to come back and hobbies and passions waiting for our time. Work fades away as we get closer to home, like a cool-down after exercise.

Nowadays, digital tools and working from home have almost removed this warm-up and cool-down, replacing it with a sudden start and stop reality. And what do you think happens with that? Let's take an analogy. If you suddenly start exercising or playing a rigorous sport without a proper warm-up, there's a high chance of getting a cramp or some other injury. Therefore, we should make subtle changes to avoid this sudden start/stop approach and ease in and out of work for our own sanity and for the sake of those around us.

A wonderful TED video I recently saw on this topic was by Guy Winch, titled 'How to Turn Off Your Work Thoughts During Your Free Time.' He outlines three practical tips for switching off when working from home:

1. **Set clear guardrails:** Define when you will stop working each night and stick to it.
2. **Create a work zone:** It is important to create a defined work zone, even if it's tiny, and work only in that space.
3. **Dress for work:** Wear work clothes while working and change out of them when you are done.

Apart from these suggestions, my personal hacks include exercising in the morning whenever possible or solving something like Sudoku or Wordle on the train to avoid jumping straight into emails and messages. While walking to the office, I think about work and what I want to get done. Then, I have breakfast at the office—a nourishing bowl of porridge—and really warm up for work by reviewing my schedule for the day before diving in. On the way back, I indulge myself with my favourite podcasts and songs as I leave the office and walk to the station. Once home, I intentionally leave my phone in random places, so I don't immediately check it. When working from home, I have made it a habit to change into work clothes (and shave) to mentally shift gears. I work at my desk for office work and at the dining table for my book writing. The one thing I haven't yet managed to do is fully switch off work at a defined time, but that's next on my agenda!

Overall, such habits will help you prepare better for both professional and personal life.

Warm up, work hard, cool down, and repeat.

Dangers of a To-Do List

We have been brought up to make to-do lists and tick off progress as we go. We have also all experienced the frustration of seeing the list somehow grow instead of shrinking by the end of the day. Then there's the unconscious urge to tick off a few things just to go home feeling a 'little' good.

The danger with such an approach is that we end up adding unimportant or non-urgent tasks to the list, completing them to see those ticks and feel good, while the important things somehow stay there forever. Herein lies the danger of the to-do list: its subtle nudging can make us unproductive rather than productive.

So, the next time you are tempted to scribble down that endless to-do list, pause for a moment and ask yourself, 'What really matters?' You might realise that the most important tasks are already front and centre in your mind—no checkboxes required. And who knows? You might even rediscover the lost art of actually getting things done instead of just listing them.

Ditch the to-do list.

Playing in the Cluttered Mine Field

Do any of the following scenarios seem relatable?

- Losing your mind searching for a file on your cluttered desktop.
- Too many files or tabs open on your laptop. An overloaded phone home screen.
- A chaotic physical desk.

The reason I am asking these questions is to highlight a correlation: a messy desktop or phone home screen often reflects a messy and inefficient mind. So, start by clearing things up. Keep your desk, desktop, and phone home screen as clean as possible and try working on one task and one file at a time.

PS: Publicly showing off your clean desktop helps. We have all been there—connecting our laptop to a projector only to be met with shocked expressions from colleagues staring at our cluttered desktops. The inevitable question follows: 'How do you ever find what you are looking for?' It's essentially a metaphor for: 'Now I know why you are so inefficient.' Now, imagine the surprise (instead of shock) when you reveal an ultra-clean desktop. Cue the impressed nods and admiring looks as you are instantly seen—and considered—as super-efficient.

Declutter your desk to boost focus and productivity.

Warren Buffet and His Empty Calendar

Did you know that Warren Buffett's calendar is, surprisingly, mostly empty? I came across this in a YouTube video that explained how he views time as his most precious resource. As Buffett wisely says, time is the one thing he cannot buy, and he chooses to use it to focus on the big things.

So, why do we need blank spaces in our calendars? From my experience, I have realised that we need our minds to be in a state of active relaxation—free from stress—to truly reflect, think, and be creative. This doesn't happen when the brain is in an active, high-stress state (beta), which is where we are when rushing from one meeting to the next. In such environments, creativity is stifled. The ideal state of mind (alpha) occurs when you are relaxed yet active. It is in this state that the brain can think creatively and solve complex problems. Therefore, it's important to create blank spaces in your calendar. Meaning, we need to make time to relax and think. Simply sitting and reflecting could be the most productive thing you do today.

My journey to reclaim control over my time was like navigating a labyrinth. At first, I was swept along by endless meetings and impulsive commitments. But observing masters of time management, I gleaned invaluable insights highlighted below:

1. **Carving Out Focus Time**

   I created sacred pockets of focus amidst the chaos, carefully aligning my schedule with my priorities. Friday afternoons became my sanctuary for connection and reflection, while holidays turned into opportunities for personal growth and exploration.

2. **Learning Discernment**

   I became selective about where to invest my time. By scrutinising my goals, ruthlessly prioritising and resisting unnecessary commitments, I reclaimed ownership of my schedule.

3. **Mastering the Power of Saying No**

   I learnt to guard my time against excessive meetings, instead leaving room for serendipitous encounters, mentorship, and self-renewal. Each moment became an investment in my long-term well-being and growth.

For those starting out, this is admittedly tough, as much of your time is dictated by others. That's why it's essential not to overload your schedule further with rigidly structured tasks. Instead, begin carving out small pockets of free time in your calendar. Let your thoughts wander and explore things you wouldn't normally do.

Clear your calendar to free your mind.

100 or 0: Stop Being a Pendulum
If you are doing something, do it properly.
Or don't do it.

If you are in, step in fully and close the door.
Or don't come in.

If you are out, leave and shut the door.
Or don't step out.

If you are thinking, think clearly.
Or don't think at all.

If you are working, focus completely.
Or don't work.

If you are chilling, relax wholeheartedly.
Or don't bother.

Now, let me take you on a journey to Ethiopia—not your typical travel story, but a tale of embracing the power of 100 per cent commitment. Picture this: I am in Ethiopia for three years, and I make a decision that most would find radical—no TV or social media. In our hyper-connected world, it felt like choosing to live on Mars. My uncle even joked that my posting to Africa was some sort of corporate exile. But here's the twist: it turned out to be the best decision of my life. Why? Because I went all in. Without the constant buzz of notifications or the hypnotic glow of a screen, I discovered something invaluable: space. Space to think, create, and truly connect. Instead of half-watching a show while scrolling on my phone, I found myself fully present at impromptu parties with colleagues, enjoying Ethiopian wine and coffee. Instead of channel surfing, I was taking walks with my wife and watching our son take his first steps.

This wasn't just about removing distractions; it was about fully committing to the life in front of me. And the results were transformative. I developed a new marketing model, introduced evidence-based strategies for building the company and its categories, and devised innovative approaches to branding, distribution, and team building. I made lifelong friends. All because I chose to go all in.

The truth is that half-measures don't work. You can't straddle two worlds and expect to fully experience either. It's like trying to stick to a diet with a fridge full of junk food—the temptation will always gnaw at you. Success doesn't require superhuman willpower; it demands creating an environment that fosters full commitment.

So, here's my challenge to you: What area of your life are you ready to go all in on? What distractions can you eliminate—not just reduce? What doors are you ready to close so you can step fully into the opportunities ahead? Remember, if you are going to do something, give it 100 per cent or don't do it at all. You might be amazed by the results.

Do it 100% or don't do it at all.

You Get What You Get, So Don't Get Upset

One of my bosses told me this a while back when I was arguing for more resources on a project: it's not about living in a fantasy where everything's perfect or sulking in a corner when it's not. Rather, it's about strapping in, looking at the cards in your hand, and saying, 'Game on'.

This little nugget of truth isn't just for show-and-tell; it's my golden-ticket advice to newbies stepping into the corporate jungle. It's also what parents tell their kids all the time. There's even a YouTube song on this—check it out later!

Now, picture this: You are eyeing that dream job, but it slips through your fingers. Or maybe you are all pumped to chase your passion, only to find out you are as good at it as a cat is at swimming. Or worse, you are the king of your domain, but it's just not lighting that spark inside you. Welcome to the club—it's called 'Life Happens'. The truth is that the MVPs of any field you have seen or heard of weren't sitting around waiting for the stars to align. They grabbed whatever piece of the puzzle they had and started putting it together, piece by gritty piece. They jumped into the fray, gave it their all, and kept moving up, step by relentless step. They didn't wait for the universe to hand them the royal flush and instead embraced pragmatism, leveraging their current situation towards success.

So, even if the desired jobs might elude you, your passions might not align with your talent, or you might excel in unenjoyable tasks, accepting these truths is crucial. I have applied this insight universally and have advised fresh entrants in the corporate realm similarly.

Play your best with what you are dealt.

Key Takeaways

- Effective work happens in efficient sprints.
- Sometimes, you must sprint when you are not up for it.
- Last-minute panic is okay—just make sure it happens in stages.
- Believe in the power of taking a complete break.
- Warm up, work hard, cool down, and repeat.
- Ditch the to-do list.
- Declutter your desk to boost focus and productivity.
- Clear your calendar to free your mind.
- Do it 100% or don't do it at all.
- Play your best with what you are dealt.

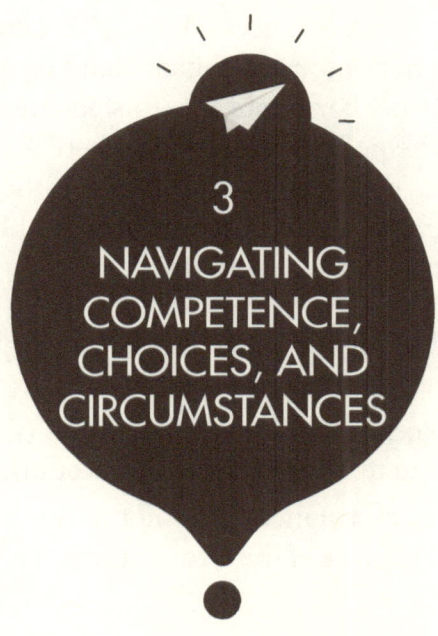

3
NAVIGATING COMPETENCE, CHOICES, AND CIRCUMSTANCES

Mastering the Variables that Shape Your Success

It is often said that choices have consequences. This is true, but in my practical experience, two additional factors play a significant role in this equation. One is more in your control, and the other less so. The chances of achieving the consequences you desire:

- Increase when you work on your competence (improving your skills, attitude, etc.).
- Fluctuate based on the circumstances you find yourself in (market conditions, company reality, etc.).

The best-case scenario for success is to continuously build your competence (within your control) and make the right choices when circumstances align. The latter may mean striking at the right moment, which could be now or later.

Throughout my corporate life, this equation has kept me grounded and helped me understand where the imbalance lies when outcomes don't meet expectations. If the consequences are not favourable, it's often because something on the left side of the equation is not working:

- It could be my competence (I failed to upskill myself or someone outperformed me).
- My choices at that time weren't right (the path I chose didn't lead to where I thought it would).
- Or the circumstances were not in my favour (I was in the wrong place at the wrong time).

In my first sales stint, my competence came to the rescue when things weren't going well. I had to roll up my sleeves, unlearn, and relearn many fundamentals. By outworking my team, I earned my stripes. In my stint in Africa, my choices played a significant role. Taking a bet on stepping outside my comfort zone to help set up my company's business in Ethiopia from scratch, alongside a few other risk-takers, proved to be an incredible confidence boost. It showed me I could start and scale a business in a completely new country. In my marketing stint in Kenya, circumstances played a major role. COVID-19 and other factors delayed my move much longer than I wanted, but in the end, it landed me a dream job at the company headquarters—an opportunity that would not have been possible had I insisted on moving earlier.

As you would expect, each situation comes with a barrage of emotions, sometimes swinging wildly from joy to frustration.

The ability to steady yourself regardless of the outcomes has, in my experience, been a key determinant of who wins the long game.

Competence + Choices + Circumstances = Consequences.

(This point was inspired by a post from the brilliant Daniel Shapero, COO of LinkedIn.)

From Workshops to Work Wins

Do you ever feel a sense of 'Oh no, not again!' every time your organisation nudges you into a training workshop or continuous learning program, or sends nuggets of wisdom to your inbox? Fear not—you are not alone.

In my experience, the learning that truly sticks is the kind that helps solve the problems you are currently facing. So, instead of sleepwalking in and out of the next training session, try focusing on learning that directly relates to the challenges you are dealing with now. You will not only deploy the learning but also retain it for a much longer time.

Looking back on my career, certain training sessions stand out. What they all had in common was their relevance to the work I was doing at the time. I still remember what was taught and how I applied it in my work to this day:

- A course for new marketers on the fundamentals of marketing.
- An advanced negotiation course during my customer marketing stint when I needed to negotiate with customers.

- A leadership course during my sales stint focused on first-time managers.
- A course on *The 7 Habits of Highly Effective People* during my sales stint when I was juggling too many tasks with too little impact.

These experiences remind me that the most impactful learning happens when it's immediately applicable.

Make learning count by focusing on what matters.

Learning with Purpose: Quality Over Quantity

You cannot read all the books in the world, watch all the TED Talks, or attend every conference—and that's okay. Over time, I have learnt that it's more valuable to focus on learning things when you can immediately put that knowledge to use. That's when it becomes a meaningful investment of your most precious and dwindling resource—time!

I have stopped worrying about CEOs who claim to read fifty-two books a year or people who comb through a zillion LinkedIn articles every week. The real question is: Have you read one thing that gave you an 'aha' moment, leading you to do things differently and achieve better results? For instance, *Good to Great* by Jim Collins redefined how I approached growth planning during my first sales stint. *How Brands Grow* by Byron Sharp left me in awe and helped me craft a marketing strategy for the Ethiopian business I was building from scratch. And *Influence: The Psychology of Persuasion* by Robert B. Cialdini transformed the way I handled stakeholder management. If I find just one book during each stint that changes the way I approach work, I consider that a win! On a related note, exploring things outside my immediate work area—like sports, movies, and fiction books—has taught me more than any subject-specific material ever could.

This approach to learning isn't just about depth but also about breadth—drawing inspiration from unexpected places to fuel creativity and innovation. Think of your brain as a creative blender, not a filing cabinet. When you toss in ingredients from different fields—sports, movies, fiction—you create a cognitive smoothie bursting with fresh perspectives and innovative ideas. This mental cross-training not only makes you more interesting at happy hour but also supercharges your problem-solving skills, boosts emotional intelligence, and helps you spot patterns others might overlook. Plus, it's way more enjoyable than slogging through another dry business book. And hey, who wouldn't want to call binge-watching Netflix 'professional development'?

Focus on reading and watching content that is directly relevant to the work you are doing and leave it at that.

Rediscovering Wisdom: The Power of Re-Reading

Maybe it's just me, but I have found immense learning and joy in re-reading books over time. When it comes to work, re-reading books acts as a refresher, a reminder, and a guide. In life, the best books I have read now carry a deeper meaning and offer more clarity as I age. And just for fun, re-reading books I enjoyed a while back has enhanced the joy, as I notice more nuances and learn why I enjoyed them in the first place.

Reading a book that truly impacts your thinking and outlook is probably better than buying lots of books, keeping them on a shelf, showing them off during video calls, and imagining that they make you more intelligent. Spiritual books come to mind instinctively here, but it could be any book. My current re-reading favourite is *The Boy, The Mole, The Fox and the Horse* by Charlie Mackesy. It has helped me stay sane through the swings of feeling wildly proud of what I have accomplished and feeling very useless about things I have yet to achieve! What's yours?

Re-read one book, then buy the next.

The Challenge of Getting Back on Track

I took a break from my exercise routine and found imaginary back problems to avoid getting back to it. I took a break from my serious reading and found enough cat videos on social media to avoid returning to it. I took my phone to bed with me during the holidays and found urgent work-related excuses to avoid kicking it out.

I have realised that taking a break from important things isn't worth it. It's not easy to restart after your car battery has gone cold. So, stay warm and stay with it.

I have tried to capture this emotion in a poem I jotted down some time ago.

It's easy to get off the track.
It's difficult to get back on.

It's easy to take your eye off the road.
It's painful to recover from an accident.

It's easy to get distracted.
It's exhausting to re-focus.

It's easy to stop.
It's tough to restart.

Don't Stop.
Keep Moving.

Stay consistent as it's hard to restart.

Knowing When to Persist and When to Let Go

In chess, if it seems inevitable that you will lose, you can accept it, shake hands, and move on. While in a sport like football, you must play on for ninety minutes even if you are badly down at the end of the first half, because there's always a chance you might make a comeback, as some epic games have shown.

In corporate life, let's say we are launching something new. If, midway through your initial launch plan, you are not where you wanted to be, it's a good time to ask yourself whether the game you are playing is chess or football. It might be that you have been outplayed and there's no realistic scenario in which you win, and hence it might be good to accept it and move on—to survive and fight another day. On the other hand, it might be that you have played badly, and your star players can still make a difference. Maybe the opponent is exhausted, and you feel you have a realistic shot at a comeback if you make some smart changes to your second-half plan. In that case, review, make the changes or substitutions, and go all out to win it. The biggest mistake, however, in my experience, is when people don't know what game they are playing and confuse decisions and outcomes as a result.

Know your game. Understand reality. Choose wisely.

This Too Shall Pass

We have all heard the famous quote: 'It is not who I am, but what I do in my weak moments that defines me.' Based on some recent introspection, I have realised that it's easy to do what is right and give my best when things are going well, and I am feeling great. But it's more important how I worked and reacted in my moments of weakness. How I showed up the next day after a presentation that didn't go well. How I reacted to a missed promotion. How I handled the pressure when the targets weren't being met. All these are different situations but with one common thread—the ability to get up, show up, and stay in the fight.

I remember in one of my marketing stints when I was part of the team that launched four different products for two brands to go up against very strong local competition. I had the logic all sorted. All the Ps of marketing ticked. The backing of a strong company with sharp marketing brains, extensive distribution muscle, and deep pockets. What could go wrong? Everything, it seems. All four products failed. Yikes! To paraphrase a famous literary line: 'All happy successes are alike; each unhappy failure is unhappy in its own way.' So, yes, the reasons were different—from misreading the strength of the competition to not having a compelling enough reason for people to change their brand, to impatience within our own team. But we learnt over time, and the brands bounced back and did very well in the years to come with a different strategy and leadership. At that time, it felt like my ambitions were being slaughtered by these failures.

But why am I telling you this story? Because I failed. And others who came after me succeeded. Did it impact my career and how I viewed it at that time? Yes. Did it eventually work out well for me? Yes, as well. Why? Because I took it in stride and realised I could either agonise over this debacle and think of myself as a poor marketer or I could blame others around me for this and deflect all blame—either way, it would spell doom for me. Maybe through luck or necessity, I stumbled upon a path of reflection and acceptance, understanding and thinking about what I could have done better myself, what I could have done to influence others, and what I could learn from the failure of what I got wrong. I promised myself to put these lessons to use in the future and that's exactly what I did. I couldn't change the past, so I learnt to accept the consequences and resolved to do better if I got a second chance. And I did get a second chance. I had to start over in some ways and prove my credentials and abilities again, and I did that by being grateful for the second chance and relishing the opportunity to prove myself. I put all my learnings to use, and it worked—I did better. The slowdown helped me speed up many years later, and I now look back at the failures and weak moments as valuable lessons—the very reason for where I am today.

The ability to stay in the fight, to keep going, to believe in yourself, and to put your hand up to ask for second chances and keep moving ahead will get you ahead. It will get you noticed, will get you second chances, and will get you to where you eventually want to go.

Keep moving forward during challenging times.

The Power of Prioritising One Significant Task

Ever had that end-of-the-day feeling where you struggle to remember what exactly you accomplished at work? Or when asked what significant thing you achieved today or yesterday, you must scratch your head to recall? If this happens far too often, maybe it's time to change how you approach your day.

Set yourself one significant thing to get done each day. Not just any task—a significant task. Something that moves your work forward, something you can end the day feeling proud of, and something that could even be part of your legacy. The kind of thing I would love for folks to talk about once I'm gone. Those 'some' things are the big things I focus on.

I don't always succeed but keeping this front and centre in my mind helps me refocus faster every time I get sidetracked with something inconsequential. You can also try the following: write down one thing you achieved at the end of each day. The more you do it, the more inspired you will be to start each day by identifying the one big thing to tackle. Over time, you will find yourself achieving more by doing less.

Reflect on the legacy you want to leave behind and get to work—there's no time to waste.

Zen and the Art of Quitting

All my life, I have been a one-company kind of person. Weird for me to talk about quitting, right? But hang on. Over two decades, I have witnessed a parade of exits and entrances at my workplace. So, what's the scoop? One harsh truth I have seen play out is that rebound jobs, like rebound relationships, often don't work out. Leaving in anger—whether it's over a missed promotion or a raise—and jumping at the next available opportunity is risky. Why? Because anger clouds your judgement, and an agitated mind rarely makes the right decisions. That's it. Nothing more complicated than that.

Here's the trick: Zen is your friend. When your mind is calm and clear, you are better equipped to make well-considered decisions. The goal isn't necessarily to stay on but to stay on long enough to figure out your next move—calmly and strategically—like Andy Dufresne in *The Shawshank Redemption*. Now, I am not suggesting you plot for nineteen years like Andy, but take the time to plan, prepare, explore your options, assess the situation, and line up some solid choices before making your move. Think of it as chess, not checkers.

But what does this really mean in practice? Let me share my story of giving up—and why it's not about quitting but about searching for what's right.

I have a long history of giving up. In high school, I gave up trying to be first in class after repeatedly coming third in exams. Why? Because I couldn't see the point of working harder on subjects that didn't interest me. After high school, I joined one of India's most prestigious colleges but dropped out after six months because the subject failed to spark any intellectual curiosity in me. Then came engineering—a degree I pursued hoping for salvation but quickly realised wasn't for me either. This time, though, I stuck with it, not out of love for the subject, but because I found other things that truly excited me: university politics, student council elections (both losing and winning), and slowly discovering what genuinely interested me. Next came business school. I started off focusing on finance but soon found myself drowning in numbers and disillusioned by the relentless focus on profiting from others' hard work. Once again, I gave up but not before discovering something that resonated: helping students secure placements through the placement office. That experience taught me more about sectors, employers, and jobs than any finance lecture ever could.

After all this 'giving up', you would think my story would end there. But here's the twist: an organisation took a chance on me because of everything I had learnt through my so-called failures. They offered me an internship, which turned into a job offer and twenty-one years later, I am still there. Not because I stopped giving up, but because I finally found what I was looking for.

Here's what I have realised: sometimes, giving up is necessary. It clears space for something better. But the key isn't just giving up; it's what you do afterward that truly counts. And one thing you should never give up is searching. Searching for what excites you. Searching for what feels right. Searching for where your competence meets opportunity and where luck, too, plays its part. Keep searching, probing, and exploring, because when you do, you might just surprise yourself with what you find.

Smart quitting = Brighter beginnings.

Luck and Skill: The Game of Life

Growing up, we all played Snakes and Ladders and Ludo. One of these games is pure luck. Sometimes you win, sometimes you lose. But even then, we tend to credit our skills when we win and blame luck only when we lose. Some folks live their lives fatalistically like this—attributing victories to their abilities and defeats to bad luck. On the other hand, the game of Ludo requires a mix of luck and skill. Luck comes first—you need a six to get out and rely on the dice to move forward. Skill comes next—you get to decide which pieces to move and when.

At the end of the day, life feels a lot like Ludo to me. Play hard and skilfully, but don't forget the role of luck in the game. Play long enough, and you will experience both wins and losses—that's just life.

Here's a short poem that captures this sentiment.

Don't be fooled by too many early wins.
Don't be disheartened by a spell of losses.

Don't be too harsh on yourself.
Don't be too full of yourself.

Be humble when you win.
Be kind to yourself when you lose.

Embrace the highs and lows of life, recognise the role of luck, and remain humble in moments of success.

Key Takeaways

- Competence + Choices + Circumstances = Consequences.
- Make learning count by focusing on what matters.
- Focus on reading and watching content that is directly relevant to the work you are doing and leave it at that.
- Re-read one book, then buy the next.
- Stay consistent as it's hard to restart.
- Know your game. Understand reality. Choose wisely.
- Keep moving forward during challenging times.
- Reflect on the legacy you want to leave behind and get to work—there's no time to waste.
- Smart quitting = Brighter beginnings.
- Embrace the highs and lows of life, recognise the role of luck, and remain humble in moments of success.

4
CRAFTING YOUR PERSONAL BRAND

What Is Your Brand?

Ever wonder what your colleagues really think of you? Or how your self-perception compares to reality in the corporate world? Let's dive into a quick self-assessment that could change how you approach your career. It's time to unpack your personal brand, and trust me, it's more revealing than your LinkedIn profile.

- What you think you are good at = Your positioning.
- What others think you are good at = Your equity.
- What you think your value is = Your dream.
- What others think your value is = Your pay cheque.

- What you think you love = Your passion.
- What others think you love = Your projection.
- What will happen if your role vanishes = What you do.
- What will happen if you vanish = What your value is.

If you are happy with the answers to these questions, great—keep doing what you are doing. If you are unhappy with the answers, great—change what you are doing. But here's the catch: change doesn't always arrive in the package we expect. Sometimes, the key to navigating revelations about your personal brand is adopting an *iko sawa* mindset. Iko sawa is a Swahili phrase I picked up while working in Kenya. It loosely translates to 'It's okay'. This simple yet profound phrase has become one of my biggest learnings. On bad days, it's a reminder that this too shall pass. On good days, it celebrates resilience. Most importantly, it teaches us to stay open to possibilities—even those that challenge our perception of our personal brand.

Let me share my iko sawa story and how it reshaped my understanding of my professional identity. Remember the self-assessment we just did? I once thought I had a firm grasp of my strengths and goals. But life had other plans. At the end of my let-me-remember-how-to-breathe story, I realised a change of surroundings might benefit my health and well-being. As if by divine intervention, an internal job opening appeared—a sales role in Ethiopia as part of a founding team to set up operations there. It checked an important box: a different environment. But it didn't align with my desire to transition away from the daily adrenaline rush of sales into a marketing role. Still, I decided to give it a shot and went for the interview.

During the interview, an unexpected twist occurred. The interviewer paused and said, 'Pawan, based on your responses and thought process, I feel you would be better suited for the head of marketing role we are also hiring for. Would you be open to interviewing for that role right now? Do you need five minutes to think it over?'

Damn and wow at the same time! I wanted the marketing job but had prepped for the sales one. Yet, here was the universe conspiring to align things for me. I told the butterflies in my stomach to settle down, said yes, took a moment to mentally reorient, and stepped into the marketing interview. This unexpected turn not only landed me the marketing role and a promotion but also kickstarted an African adventure that transformed my career and life perspective. It taught me that sometimes, our true strengths, passions, and opportunities reveal themselves in the most surprising ways.

The lesson? While self-awareness is essential, being open to unexpected opportunities and others' perspectives on your abilities can lead to rewarding new paths. Your personal brand isn't just what you think it is; it's also shaped by how others see you and by the chances you take when the unexpected comes knocking.

So, as you reflect on your self-assessment, remember iko sawa. It's okay if your perception doesn't match reality. It's okay if unexpected opportunities disrupt your career plan. Embrace the journey of discovering and reshaping your personal brand. Because in the end, as they say in Swahili, iko sawa—it's all okay.

Evaluating your personal brand unlocks career potential.

What Problem Are You Solving?

Having a workplace superpower doesn't mean leaping tall buildings in a single bound. Instead, it's about identifying and solving problems that leave your colleagues scratching their heads. It's about being the person who sees solutions where others see roadblocks. Let's dive into how you can uncover and harness this unique ability to become the office hero (cape optional).

Ask yourself these key questions:

- What problems am I solving that no one else is tackling?
- Am I solving these problems better than anyone else?
- Is there a real need for the problems I solve?
- How exactly am I solving them, and can I improve my approach?
- Are people aware that I solve these problems?
- Do they recognise me as the expert in this area?

Answering these questions will help you pinpoint your superpower and ensure it's not just useful but also noticed. Remember that in the corporate jungle, your superpower isn't just a neat party trick; it's your ticket to becoming indispensable. The ability to solve problems effectively and uniquely will set you apart.

Discover your superpower by identifying the unique problems only you can solve.

Building Your Brand

Much like any brand, the building blocks for creating your personal brand are the same. Let me outline four of these building blocks here:

1. **Functional Benefit**

    What is your core functional skill that you bring to the table, like the product or service that anchors a brand? Know this well. In my experience, this first step is the most difficult in today's world, where skills and experiences are changing and evolving rapidly. Asking people who have worked with you to describe you is a simple yet effective starting point.

2. **Emotional Benefit**

    How do you make people feel when you work with them? How do others describe working with you? Do they feel respected, valued, happy, and relaxed or unhappy and stressed? Do they feel hope or despair, trust or suspicion? We are driven by our emotions, and at the end of the day, how you make someone feel can make a big difference to your brand.

3. **Brand Say = Brand Do**

    This is the third and most important building block. What you say, you must do. And only what you do, you must say. Simple yet so difficult to live up to. It's like we are taught to overpromise and underdeliver when the opposite is a better and more pragmatic approach. Brands are built on trust, so if there's one muscle you should focus on building, it's the 'say = do' muscle.

4. Awareness

If no one knows about you, all the above don't really matter. It's probably an area I have struggled with personally as well. Hence, I have learnt a lot from my experiences and experiments. First, I have learnt that it helps immensely to engage with more and more people. This can be achieved by expanding the scope of your work, raising your hand to take on more work, showcasing your work where possible, and helping others with theirs. Second, you need to matter in the moments that matter. That one big presentation, the one big market visit, the chance encounter with a senior leader—these moments count. You have got to showcase your work in a way that leaves a lasting impression. Be like super glue, not a post-it note that falls off the wall after a while. Think, prepare, be ready, and matter when it matters.

Strong functional benefit + Strong emotional benefit + No say-do gap + High awareness = Strong brand.

How Is Your Brand Health?

Not all of us remember to do annual health check-ups. When things go wrong, we have no choice but to go for check-ups, listen to doctors, and follow their advice to get better. We might do regular check-ups for a while after that, but for most people, it becomes irregular again. That's just how we are—generally optimistic.

For those of us in marketing, regular brand health checks are the norm. For businesses, audits to check the overall health of the company are also common. That is how businesses tend to be—generally cautious.

Now, regarding your 'personal brand', which one are you: optimistic or cautious? My experience suggests that being cautious and checking in regularly with your boss, peers, and subordinates about what they think of you is worthwhile. At the very least, it will confirm your own assessment. If there are surprises, it gives you the confidence to address them with solid evidence. A 360-degree feedback, even if not mandatory in your organisation, will be immensely useful for building your personal brand.

For me, some of the most impactful shifts in my career happened when I did my brand health checks. Some occurred during annual appraisal discussions, others in opportunistic car rides with bosses, some during mid-year 360-degree feedback sessions, and a few in late-night chats during office off-sites. I still remember a few vividly, one of them being at the end of my second sales stint as a regional sales manager. I wanted a promotion and a shift to marketing, and I had the chance to speak to my skip-level boss during a car ride to the airport. Because it was a short ride, the feedback came fast and furious (not literally). He said, 'You can get a promotion in sales, or you can move to marketing without a promotion, but the probability of getting both is low. You decide. Bye.' I didn't have much time to respond immediately; my words were caught by my nervousness, so the ride's end was a blessing in disguise.

Later, after getting over my gratitude for the crystal-clear feedback, I felt dejected for not getting the desired outcome. The realities of making stark choices became apparent, and I decided to stick with sales and pursue a promotion. I realised then that choices and circumstances have consequences. I applied for a sales job in Ethiopia but, strangely, ended up with a marketing role during the interview. The point is that a timely check revealed the reality of my brand positioning and helped me make better choices. All in all, make sure to check your brand health regularly and be aware of your reality. You may like what you see, or you may not, but you won't regret it.

Regular personal brand health check-up = No long-term personal brand surprises or shocks.

Brands Cannot Fail but You Can

Brands are built on trust and a promise. When you decide to spend your money on a brand to consume or experience it, it better deliver on that trust and promise. If it doesn't, you don't buy it again—once bitten, twice shy. Not only that, in today's world, you tell others not to spend their money on the brand.

Now, for your personal brand, things are different, and you are lucky they are. We make mistakes, we aren't as consistent as we would like to be, and we sometimes fail in things we set out to do. And yet, that's okay. How we fail and move ahead, how we learn and improve, these aspects paradoxically define our human brand, unlike products where failure is the end of the road. Remember this difference, embrace your humanness, and build your brand around your strengths and weaknesses, your confidence and vulnerability, your successes and failures.

I was recently reviewing some of my annual appraisals over the years to look for patterns. I did find some related to my strengths—being strategic, connecting the dots, and being a strong intellectual thinker, among others. Then, I found something interesting. This was linked to my areas of development. Interestingly, there was no pattern here. This had me stumped for a bit until I finally spotted the pattern. Every time I received feedback on an area of development, I tried my best to work on it. Whether you call it my 'Indian good-school-boy-wanting-to-impress-the-teacher syndrome' or the corporate necessity to progress, it worked out that I was able to improve on these areas and get a passing mark by the next appraisal cycle, leading to those issues no longer being raised. And something else took its place. That's when it struck me that we may be super good at a few things that are our core strengths, and in our areas of weakness, we may or may not end up becoming experts, but we can work to get better at them through conscious effort.

Don't strive to be a perfect product brand; instead, embrace an authentic, imperfect human brand.

It Is the Work That Counts

What you do is important to the team, the boss, and the organisation. Otherwise, why would your role exist? And you are in that role because the boss believes you can perform the prescribed work well. But be aware that ultimately, it's the work that matters. Don't confuse this with thinking that you matter more than the contribution you bring. It's what you bring to the table that counts. In return, you should expect fair compensation—wages, respect, work-life balance, etc.—making it a fair trade.

The challenge arises when an employee starts believing they matter more than their work or that they are indispensable. It's like hanging onto a balloon that is floating upward; it will eventually burst, bringing you back down with a thud. Equally challenging is when the organisation (or boss) focuses solely on the work and neglects things like respect, work-life balance, or managing expectations. That's like stretching a rubber band; it will eventually snap. This is a good reminder to check in with yourself and your boss as you continue building your brand.

Your brand is your work.

Brands Need Advertising

It is true that your brand is your work, but it is equally true that your brand exists in the minds of others. Communicating your work to the world is a critical part of building your personal brand. Here are three practical tips:

1. **Have an Elevator Pitch**

    Introduce yourself and your work in a concise, compelling way. Write it. Re-write it. Practice it. I have learnt late in life how important this is as you rarely get a second chance to make a first impression. A sharp and emotional pitch sticks like super glue; a weak one falls away like a post-it note on a wall.

2. **Dress Sharp**

    Maybe I am old school, but so are most bosses, I suspect. I am not advocating rigid dress codes but showing care in how you present yourself—whether meeting your boss, a client, or your team—projects attention to detail. And that care creates an emotional connection, which sticks.

3. **Build a Portfolio**

   A deck, a video, or even a note outlining what you achieved and how you did it can make all the difference. Think of how a wedding photographer or interior designer showcases their portfolio to demonstrate their calibre. Over time, you will forget many of your own achievements, and that's a shame. Keep a journal or write an end-of-project note to yourself. It helps.

One of my favourite elevator pitches in a past role was: 'I work on tomorrow.' A bit tacky, maybe, but it got people curious enough to ask for details, which opened the door to share more. Many CEOs use similar approaches. You have probably seen it too where a CEO might describe themselves as the 'chief energy officer' or something similar to succinctly convey their focus and passion.

I once had a boss—now a well-known MD/CEO—who described himself as a 'simple soap salesman.' Initially, I found it amusing until I realised it was his way of staying grounded. It reminded him to focus on what mattered most: helping us sell more effectively in the market. This is the real power of a good elevator pitch: it reflects what you love doing, what energises and excites you, and where your focus lies. It speaks volumes about you.

PS: Perfecting your elevator pitch is like tuning a violin—every note must resonate with precision and harmony. Rehearse in front of a mirror or record yourself on your phone. With practice, you become a maestro fine-tuning your masterpiece.

After all, every interaction is a stage, and you, the performer, must seize the spotlight and deliver a flawless performance.

(I must thank my son for inspiring this violin metaphor. Watching him practice and perform one day sparked this thought, and it felt fitting.)

Advertise consistently, continuously, and conspicuously.

It's Not the Job, It's You

Ever notice how some people consistently land the best opportunities while others struggle to get noticed? The truth is, it's not about the jobs themselves; it's about the mindset and actions of the individuals behind them. Success hinges more on your effort and attitude than on any title or position. Shifting focus from external circumstances to internal drive can be transformative. To illustrate this, here's a short reflection that captures the essence of this idea:

There are no dream jobs,
only people who dream big.

There are no famous jobs,
only people who achieve remarkable things.

There are no easy jobs,
only people who work hard to make things look easy.

There are no amazing teams,
only people who work well to make the team amazing.

There are no career-limiting jobs,
only career-limiting actions.

It's never about the job;
it's always about you.

It's not what the job gives you but what you make of it.

(The inspiration for this section was shared by Ruchi Agrawal Marella during a conversation following my annual appraisal discussion.)

Clapping for Your Own Magic?

The magician knows it's not magic, but a carefully staged and rehearsed trick. The kids in the audience don't. They clap and go wild! But what happens if the magician starts believing it's magic too? What then? Eventually . . . disaster.

It's the same with us. There's the stuff you tell others to look good, the stuff others tell you to flatter you (especially if you are the boss), and then there's the stuff you know deep down is true. This includes plain unvarnished facts—the kind you only share with your barber or hairstylist. Thus, it is crucial to realise that the most dangerous illusion is the one you create for yourself. It's easy to get caught up in the applause, the promotions, or the fancy job titles. But true growth comes from seeing past the smoke and mirrors of your own success. So, take a moment to step behind the curtain of your career. Are you still practising your craft, or have you started believing in your own hype? After all, the best performers are the ones who never stop rehearsing, even when the audience thinks they are flawless.

So, when was the last time you did an honest self-assessment? Maybe it's time for a haircut!

Be honest in your self-assessment.

Some Things Never Go out of Fashion

One of the nicest gestures I remember from one of my bosses was his habit of writing thank-you notes to the families of top performers. This was during one of my sales stints, and he would take out his old-fashioned, regal ink pen and write detailed, personalised, handwritten notes to the immediate family of the team member—parents, spouse, or others. He would then ensure the notes were sent to them.

Imagine the joy, surprise, and pride the family members felt upon receiving such a thoughtful note, and how appreciated and valued the team member must have felt as well. A simple thank-you note, written and delivered with care and respect, had a profound impact. It fostered deep loyalty, created a sense of pride, and even built my boss his own fan club! I know he continues to do this even now, and it has become one of his brand hallmarks—something that will stay with him forever.

Building on this idea of thoughtful gestures and respectful behaviours, here are some simple yet impactful practices that can leave a lasting impression

- Be on time, whether you are the intern or the boss.
- Say 'please' before asking for something.
- Write thank-you notes and send as many as you can.
- Hold the door open for everyone.
- Push your chair back in place after every meeting.

- Finish on time, especially on Mondays and Fridays.
- Apologise when you make a mistake.
- Wait for your turn to speak.
- Keep your mouth closed when eating or listening.

Brand building includes embracing the lessons from your five-year-old self.

Key Takeaways

- Evaluating your personal brand unlocks career potential.
- Discover your superpower by identifying the unique problems only you can solve.
- Strong functional benefit + Strong emotional benefit + No say-do gap + High awareness = Strong brand.
- Regular personal brand health check-up = No long-term personal brand surprises or shocks.
- Don't strive to be a perfect product brand; instead, embrace an authentic, imperfect human brand.
- Your brand is your work.
- Advertise consistently, continuously, and conspicuously.
- It's not what the job gives you but what you make of it.
- Be honest in your self-assessment.
- Brand building includes embracing the lessons from your five-year-old self.

Part II
You and Others

'The strength of the pack is the wolf, and the strength of the wolf is the pack.'
—Raksha, *The Jungle Book*

Imagine this: I was a new, zealously determined area sales manager, responsible for regional sales and leading a team. We had a distributor who wasn't meeting our standards but was a local heavyweight—tough to handle. In a bold (and risky) move, I sent a team leader to address the issue. Next thing I know, my team leader is locked up in the distributor's warehouse! No MBA course had prepared me for this.

Frantically rushing to the scene, I too ended up locked in the warehouse. The distributor demanded a written assurance that he would remain our main distributor. Petrified would be an understatement. My thoughts swung between mundane concerns like where to pee and philosophical musings on how I had landed myself in this surreal situation. In a panic, I called my boss. His experience shone through. He instructed me to draft a carefully worded statement to appease the distributor without compromising our standards. But that wasn't all. My boss had also called our local factory manager for backup. Soon, a group of enthusiastic factory workers arrived, restoring the balance of power. Together, we crafted the statement, defused the situation, and managed to get out safely. Later, my boss demonstrated the thoughtful art of problem-solving: asking the right questions, involving diverse perspectives, and finding pragmatic solutions.

This experience became a masterclass in leadership and teamwork—lessons I have carried throughout my career. This incident perfectly encapsulates the core themes we will explore in Part II of this book:

1. **The Art of Self-Expression**
    My initial communication with the distributor clearly missed the mark. In this part, we will explore why people often walk away from the same meeting with vastly

different interpretations and how to disagree gracefully to avoid such escalations.

2. **The Power of Asking the Right Questions**
   My boss's approach to resolving the crisis highlighted the importance of this skill. We will discuss how to identify what isn't happening or changing and master the challenging yet essential art of asking open-ended questions.

3. **Successful Teamwork**
   The resolution, involving factory workers, demonstrated the wisdom of collective effort. We will uncover the secrets of effective collaboration, addressing power dynamics and common team challenges.

4. **Navigating Workplace Culture**
   This warehouse drama served as a stark reminder that sanitized office environments don't prepare us for real-life challenges. We will discuss how workplace culture shapes daily experiences and how you can foster a positive culture, even if you are not in a leadership role.

Through practical, everyday office scenarios and lessons drawn from experiences, Part II will equip you with tools to master communication, collaboration, and cultural navigation in your workplace. In most companies, culture is the ultimate differentiator, and understanding how to thrive within it is key to success.

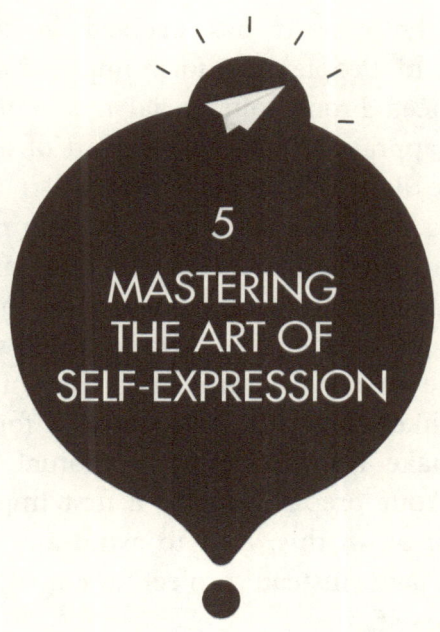

5
MASTERING THE ART OF SELF-EXPRESSION

Life's a Pitch

Whether it's a new colleague, vendor, interview, or pitch, a great first impression is an essential foundation to build everything on. Thus, it's vital to take the time to prepare. Know who you are meeting and think about what they might want. Craft your introduction and elevator pitch. You have worked hard, you have got a great idea, you are diligent, or you have got good grades—whatever the message, prepare to convey it effectively.

That said, it's important to clarify that this preparation isn't about being disingenuous or simply telling the other person what they want to hear. Rather, it's about ensuring that your key takeaway message lands exactly as you intend. Remember, there is no second chance to make a first impression.

However, the context has evolved in today's hyper-connected world. People often form impressions of you long before you meet. From your social media posts and past performance appraisals to what a friend of a friend might say, first impressions can begin to form well in advance of the actual meeting. So, while the importance of making a strong impression during your first interaction remains, it's no longer the complete picture. Hence, be aware of the impressions you have already created in the world; these will likely find their way to the person you are meeting. They might check your social media likes and comments, conduct formal reference checks, or make informal calls to mutual acquaintances for insights. Your preparation for a first impression needs to account for all of this. Aim to avoid any dissonance or inconsistency and instead project a consistent, coherent picture of yourself.

Let me share what I do, not as a suggestion, but as an example of my approach. My public social media presence is limited to LinkedIn, where I focus on calm networking and politely sharing my thoughts. I either stay off other platforms entirely or maintain private or dummy profiles to understand platform dynamics and professional insights. For my personal life, I keep it intentionally private, reserving its excitement for those closest to me. I also value my trusted network, i.e., people I have worked with over the years. I try to stay in touch, with varying degrees of success. Those I have maintained connections with continue to be great references and sources of support.

Lastly, I diligently try to help everyone who reaches out to me. I believe in good karma (yes, I am a believer!), and I have seen it return to me in the form of blessings and kind words that find their way to the right people at the right time.

Remember, there is no second chance to make a first impression.

My English Is Not Your English

Ever found yourself scratching your head, wondering why the other person isn't understanding what you are saying, while they are likely feeling the same about you? One, often overlooked, reason for this is that English is not the native language for many of us. Even for those who are native speakers, words and sentences can carry different meanings depending on the context in their country or company. And it may sound amusing, but when this is combined with big egos and serious topics, it can quickly escalate into heated debates and disagreements, even on matters where there might have been alignment all along! Such are the strange ways of the corporate world.

My key learnings on this subject are as follows:

- Facts, figures, and actual demonstrations help, as they transcend language barriers.
- Repeating what you have heard and understood to the other person can be invaluable. Similarly, asking others to replay what they understood works wonders.

Communicate clearly and ensure understanding.

Stop Using Difficult Words

Recently, I saw a book titled *Difficult Words*. This is a book to avoid if you are aiming to persuade others or help them understand things. However, you will still find a significant following of this esteemed book in many companies. Followers of this book use complicated phrases and difficult words that could mean nothing or anything! And if the subject is even mildly technical, difficult words are complemented by the use of acronyms, random statistics, and data points, all designed to psychologically intimidate you and tilt the power balance in their favour.

Over time, I have realised that the people who cannot explain something in simple terms are simply not good at their job. It is now a filter I use regularly when engaging with others. Remember, it is the job of the person presenting or convincing to do so in a way that you understand. All you need to do is keep an open mind.

Simple words = Clear understanding.

Saying the Right Thing, the Right Way

Ever feel like you are speaking a different language in meetings? Or that your brilliant ideas seem to evaporate the moment they leave your mouth? Don't worry—you are not alone. Welcome to the wild world of corporate communication, where 'how' you say something is just as important as 'what' you say.

One simple but critical lesson I have learnt in my career is that to get your way, you must not only say the right things but also say them in the right way and at the right time. It took me a while to figure this out, but now it seems so obvious (Hindsight really is 20/20, isn't it?). But there's the catch: even knowing this, I still mess up in the heat of the moment. It's like preparing for a big game and then forgetting all your plays as soon as you step onto the field. Sound familiar? So, what's the secret sauce to remedy this situation? It comes down to how much time I have spent thinking about the 'what' and the 'how'—the content and the audience—and how much I have prepped and rehearsed.

Think of it like this: your ideas are the star of the show, but your delivery is the spotlight that makes them shine. Here's a challenge for you: before your next big meeting or presentation, take a moment to consider not just what you want to say, but how your audience might receive it. Are you speaking their language? Are you addressing their concerns? Are you using the right tone? In the corporate world, it's not just about having good ideas; it's about making those ideas stick. Let me illustrate this with a story from the highlands of Addis Ababa.

Picture a corporate meeting room in a hotel where my team and I were earnestly trying to sell a bold idea to transform it into a big business for the organization. After a few lukewarm attempts with logical facts, charts, projections, business cases, and Excel sheets going nowhere, I knew I had to try something different. Desperate times call for desperate measures. I decided to abandon the usual dry, corporate approach and switched to storytelling, drawing inspiration from my childhood love of movies and fiction novels. My primary objective became to stir up emotions.

I created a presentation titled 'Back to the Future', framing our message as a journey back in time to learn and build strong business foundations. Each chapter was named after a movie, complete with a poster, telling a compelling sub-story. I combined stakeholder engagement with real human stories, showing the tangible impact of our work. By demonstrating that doing well as a company also meant doing good in the communities where we operated, I transformed abstract statistics into emotional, compelling narratives.

The result? That presentation sparked emotions, secured the funding and support we needed, and became a cornerstone of our journey. It proved that clear, passionate communication could transform scepticism into enthusiasm. The main lesson here is that expressing yourself effectively—whether outlining expectations to your team or presenting ideas to your boss—is a skill worth mastering. It's like sharpening a blade that cuts through confusion and misunderstanding. When your ideas resonate emotionally, they are not just heard; they are remembered.

So, are you ready to level up your communication game and make your ideas not just understood, but truly felt?

Say right things in the right way to get your way.

When 'Obvious' Isn't Enough

Every now and then, we hear phrases like 'I thought it was assumed' or 'We thought it was obvious'. However, it's important to recognise that what seems clear to us may not be understood by others. It is best not to assume and to check, rather than leaving things to interpretation. Sometimes, what feels obvious needs to be explained or clarified. Therefore, it's always a good idea to elaborate on what we mean instead of leaving things to imagination or inference. Doing so will not only make sure effective communication Doing so will not only ensure effective communication but also build a lot more trust, which, in turn, is the best foundation for working together to achieve great things.

The place I uncovered this was in Ethiopia. I heard everything, from whether Ethiopians speak French to whether I needed to take water with me in my suitcase when I was flying into Ethiopia during my time there. When I was asked to build a business case for the country with some big numbers, my initial assumptions got the better of me. I got stuck in a pessimistic place at first, unable to see how it could be done. Then, I stopped assuming and started checking—checking on how other countries grew, checking on some amazing companies that already had big businesses in Ethiopia, looking at interesting facts like Ethiopia Airlines being the most profitable airline in Africa, Ethiopia having the largest quantity of cattle in Africa, or even Ethiopia never being colonised and charting its own destiny. Many more 'aha' moments later, as facts started triumphing over assumptions (and biases and blind spots), we were able to build a strong business case that convinced the powers that be to invest in the country. The rest, as they say, is history.

Stop assuming and start asking.

Clarity Through Writing, Not Slides

The more I am forced to write on the entire idea, the more difficult it becomes. It requires a high clarity of thinking and expression to say exactly what you want to say. Once you write it, it's there and not open to interpretation. On the other hand, a PowerPoint presentation is like a magical trick to hide your lack of clarity. It leaves things open to interpretation and imagination with images and a few bold phrases that could mean anything or nothing. So, make charts, use images, and be creative in decks, but only after you have achieved clarity of thinking and expression by writing it down clearly.

Now, I have done my fair share of PowerPoints—some even wow-worthy, if I may say so myself—but even those wow presentations only served to make people remember the session or the topic, not much more. The real deal is what you write, explain, and lay bare in black and white. Try it. It's tougher than it sounds but easier than finding that wow image for the slide.

Forget the PPT—go with a Word doc instead.

Meeting Etiquette: Accept or Decline but Communicate

With so much work happening via virtual meetings nowadays, it's time to ask yourself: are you accepting or declining meetings, or just not doing anything about the invite? If you accept or decline (with comments, if possible, as that will be polite and good business etiquette), it helps the other person plan. If you don't do anything (neither accept nor decline), imagine the chaos in the meeting as no one is sure if you are joining or not. Consider the loss of credibility for yourself as a professional, and this erosion of credibility builds over time, making you less reliable and, consequently, less trustworthy. When that happens, it's game over.

Don't let indecision damage your professionalism.

Repeating Yourself Doesn't Help

In my experience, the more I hear phrases like 'As per my last email', 'As we discussed before', and 'As I had mentioned earlier' being used, the higher the probability that the task hasn't been completed. The reason being that why would you need to reiterate something repeatedly unless there's a lack of alignment or clarity? And if that's the case, just repeating yourself won't solve it!

Parents of young kids know this aspect all too well. Repeating isn't going to solve the problem and instead, addressing it with creativity, trying different approaches, asking questions, changing your perspective, and encouraging honest, safe conversations will make the difference. I consciously try to avoid using these phrases, and when I do, it's always a sign of an issue on my end. Think about this the next time you catch yourself using these phrases!

Stop repeating yourself.

Focus or Hocus-Pocus?

How often do we hear the phrase 'Focus on this to make it better' in office meetings? But have you ever stopped to consider if it's being interpreted the right way? What does 'focus' really mean? The truth is, this phrase can mean different things to different people. Simply put, it's often used as a corporate cop-out when there's no clear solution to a problem, with the hope that simply saying 'focus' will somehow make everything better. One might as well say hocus pocus! Thus, it's always better to specify the exact tasks you want done. Clear actions. Tangible steps. Practical tasks that someone can act on. Then you might get somewhere. As a byproduct of this, you also earn the respect of the people who work with you and for you.

I remember during my various sales stints, we used to do focused 'sales drives'—an intense effort to increase sales when there was an issue. And sometimes it worked, sometimes it didn't. Digging deeper, I found that the meaning of 'focus' was different for different people, and rightfully so. The actions everyone took were different, and not everything worked. For example, if someone just sold more than the usual volume to a retailer and did nothing else to drive higher output from the store, the next time you visited, unsurprisingly, you got no orders because the stock from the last time was still sitting there.

When I gently changed my approach to understand why sales were low and zeroed in on a few reasons, like low demand, low distribution, monetary challenges for distributors, and poor inventory planning, we could break down the actions into different buckets depending on the problem and allocate the right resources to solve it, whether it was smarter consumer promotions, increasing distribution, or solving cash flow problems. And occasionally, just focusing also helped—strangely enough. This was almost always tied to a person being distracted by other things in their life or facing challenges that troubled them. In these cases, focusing as an action plan meant understanding their problems and helping solve them in the right way to get their mindset back to work planning and executing.

So, when someone asks you to focus, ask for specifics. It will help you. And when you ask someone to focus, be specific.

Stop focusing aimlessly and start being precise.

What Do You Have?

Ever wondered why some ideas spark immediate action while others fizzle out in the conference room? The secret often lies in how you frame your thoughts. Let's break it down:

- I have a dream → Inspires.
- I have a plan → Drives action.
- I have a view → ?

Remember, in the corporate world, it's not just about having ideas; it's about presenting them in a way that inspires action. Turning your experience and passion into a vision and building a plan around it is challenging but deeply rewarding. On the other hand, merely sharing a view—without direction or purpose—is like shouting into the void, making little to no impact.

So, before you speak up in your next meeting, ask yourself: Are you sharing a dream, presenting a plan, or just offering a view? Your answer could be the key to unlocking your influence and making your voice truly heard.

What do you have? A dream, a plan, or just a view?

Key Takeaways

- Remember, there is no second chance to make a first impression.
- Communicate clearly and ensure understanding.
- Simple words = Clear understanding.
- Say right things in the right way to get your way.
- Stop assuming and start asking.
- Forget the PPT—go with a Word doc instead.
- Don't let indecision damage your professionalism.
- Stop repeating yourself.
- Stop focusing aimlessly and start being precise.
- What do you have? A dream, a plan, or just a view?

6
THE POWER OF ASKING THE RIGHT QUESTIONS

How You Doin'?

'How you doin'?' Joey made this line iconic in *Friends*, but it's probably the best first question to ask in any work interaction. How we are feeling has a strong correlation with how we perform at work, and understanding what is going on with the other person is hugely helpful and beneficial and is a great way to build team trust and bonding.

During my time in Africa, we learnt a technique for this in a work training program. It is called a 'Check-In', and it is exactly what it says: a 'check' to get you 'in' to the meeting. We now start most of our meetings with a check-in. A check-in to see how everyone is feeling from a personal and work perspective. Each person goes around and speaks for a minute about what is on their mind and how their frame of mind is as they enter the meeting, both literally and mentally. And as you build a circle of trust within the team, people slowly unveil themselves and share the truth. When that happens, amazing things happen. It could be someone talking about their child being unwell the night before, leaving them exhausted and unable to get a good night's rest, or someone saying they are distracted because they are expecting an important update on their parent's travel, explaining why they are continuously checking their phone.

Knowing what is going on with someone can make such a big difference in the meeting. Now that you know, you can work with that understanding and kindness to make the session more productive, and more importantly, avoid making assumptions and misjudgements about why someone is behaving in a certain way.

Know that everything at work is personal to some extent. Try building a circle of authentic understanding within the team and creating a culture where sharing personal matters, safely, is encouraged. It will make a remarkably big difference in how the team comes together to work and achieves greater results than you thought possible.

Ask more often: 'How you doin'?'

Ready, Set, Go

Read and ready—that is the approach the best bosses I have worked with take when preparing for meetings and tackling work in general. Come what may, they read up on pre-reads, think through desired outcomes, make notes on key points and questions, ask for and bring in different viewpoints, and bring energy into the room for the meeting and work in general.

When you see someone and think they were 'born ready' for their role, it's worth noting that they weren't. What sets them apart is the effort they put in behind the scenes. They burn the midnight oil more than others. They grind through what needs to be done to be ready. They work smarter with their time, focusing and cutting out distractions when it's work time. They get in the zone when it matters most. This level of preparation applies equally to meetings and all other aspects of their work. They are (well) read and (very) ready. The question is, are you?

The best bosses and team members I have worked with have all had different hacks for managing this. For instance:

- One of my bosses would block thirty minutes before the meeting to read or re-read the pre-reads, ensuring everything was fresh in his mind.
- Another would share the pre-reads with team members and gather comments, allowing for a broader perspective in their input.
- Another person I know printed out a large A3 paper and diligently made notes for key points with diagrams and graphs, as that is how his mind worked.
- One individual simply and unemotionally cancelled the meeting if the team didn't send the pre-read forty-eight hours before the meeting.
- Another mandated a specific pre-read template that made information easier for them to comprehend (a luxury they could afford as the boss!).

So, no matter the situation, make sure that you are well-read and ready. It might not be easy, but nothing good was ever easy.

PS: Yes, generative AI tools can help you summarise heaps of documents, but please do not do that if the tool you are using is public and the data you are uploading is private.

Be (well) read and (very) ready.

What Is Missing May Matter Most

In today's fast-paced world, where change is constant, if everything suddenly goes quiet, it's probably not a time to relax but to be on high alert. It is a sign that someone is probably getting ready to do something big, announce something new, or change the status quo in some way.

The first step to counter this is spotting the lull in activity. That is where many of us struggle. Our instinct—and by consequence, organisational instinct—is to wake up and spot danger only after it arrives, then scramble to react. So, ask yourself and everyone around you these counterintuitive questions:

- What is it out there that you are not seeing?
- What is not happening?
- What is oddly absent?
- What has suddenly stopped?

Assessing these things smartly will help you prepare for what is coming your way. You will be better equipped to do what is needed and won't be surprised when the onslaught happens.

It reminds me of a situation we faced in Kenya. The portfolio I was responsible for included soaps. One of the challenges we encountered was that our bathing soaps were 'getting over' too fast. We started by checking the formulations and product specifications, and everything seemed fine. What could be the reason for this feedback? Maybe consumers could tell us. We went on multiple consumer home visits (CHVs, as we used to fondly call them) across the country.

Finally, the elusive 'aha' moment came when we asked to see the bathrooms of folks and how the soaps were stored. The answer lay there—in something that was not there. Many homes we visited did not store the soap in a soap dish after use; instead, they kept it on a ledge where it continued to be wet. This led to it becoming mushy and eventually wearing off faster than we had anticipated. This clear problem definition led to two solutions: one focused on making the soap formulation better to withstand this reality, and the other on launching a consumer promotion where we packed the soap inside a branded, transparent, closed soap dish. It turned out to be a huge hit, and the soap dish also ended up having multiple uses around the house! Sometimes, you must keep a keen eye on what is not there, what is not happening, and magic happens.

PS: The technical learnings aside, it's not easy to keep checking for what is not happening in a world where so much is changing. Everyone—from your boss to your team members—will ask you about the latest trend or tool and what you are changing, so it takes a bit of confidence in the face of uncertainty, a bit of sticking to your guns, a few deep breaths, and some prayers for this to work!

Keep an eye out for what is not there.

The 90-10 Rule

The 90-10 rule suggests that 90 per cent of the time should be spent identifying the root cause of a problem, and only 10 per cent on planning the solution. Yet, many people reverse this ratio. Pressure to deliver results and pressure from the boss often lead to folks spending little time digging below the surface to find the root issue. As a result, they rush to develop multiple solutions and deploy them using a 'try and see' method, wasting more time and money, and, unless they are exceptionally lucky, making little progress. Thus, it's crucial to build resilience and allow yourself time to get to the root cause of the problem, even though it might make you feel nervous, as it will make all the difference.

Back in Africa, I learnt this lesson while working on the launch of our hair care brand. It took us a few tumultuous years to go from initial thinking to final launch. Seems oddly slow when you first think about it, right? But therein lies the learning. Those long years weren't spent twiddling our thumbs. Instead, they were spent getting the right people to lead the project first—people with relevant practical experience and the ability to work in a very uncertain and fluid environment. Then came the time spent deeply understanding the consumer pain points and experimenting with different formulations and concepts, since none of the products on the market were really solving their problems. This involved evaluating how to manufacture, launch, and sell in a way that was viable from an end-to-end perspective, from raw materials sourcing to final pricing, all in an environment where things were changing rapidly, from inflation to government rules to global challenges, while the consumer problem remained the same.

After many 'No, not yet' responses to the classic question, 'Are we there yet?', we finally launched, and it was a huge success! We knew that if it was difficult for us, it was difficult for others as well. But the bigger, long-lasting lessons were the importance of dedicating time to thoroughly define the problem and solution before moving swiftly into execution once the thinking is clear. Equally important was hiring the right people, valuing progress over speed, consistency over bursts of effort, and prioritising thoughtful planning over rushing into action.

Much later, I came across the book *How Big Things Get Done* by Bent Flyvbjerg and Dan Gardner, which brilliantly outlines why the 90-10 approach works. As they say in the book, 'Put enormous care and effort into planning to ensure that delivery is swift and smooth. Think slow, act fast. That's the secret of success.'

90% analysis + 10% solution = 100% results.

Unlocking Deeper Insights Through Thoughtful Questions

We are wired to avoid or delay pain, to seek easy answers, and generally to try to get things done the easy way. However, things at work are rarely that simple. One of the ways to avoid falling into this trap is to ask the right questions.

1. **Avoid the Yes/No Trap**

    When reviewing your team, asking questions like 'The target will happen, right?' will likely result in a quick 'Yes', simply because the person being asked wants to avoid a long discussion. A better approach is to ask more pointed questions that don't have a simple yes or no answer. For example, asking, 'How much of the target will you achieve?' invites a deeper conversation and provides more useful insights.

2. **The 5 Whys**

   Another useful technique is the 5 Whys. Asking 'why' multiple times helps peel back the layers of a problem and get to the root cause. This is a well-known Japanese technique which is simple yet powerful. As a leader, using this method encourages your team to think critically, rather than falling back on rehearsed answers. It promotes real problem-solving.

3. **The 5Ws and H of Work**

   To ensure you are approaching a problem the right way, ask the following:

   - What problem are you solving? Is it significant enough to warrant attention?
   - Who else is working on solving it? Are you uniquely positioned to tackle this problem?
   - Who are you solving it for? Do they truly want or need the solution?
   - How will you solve it? Are there multiple approaches?
   - Why should people believe in your solution? Why will you succeed where others might not?
   - When and Where can people learn about and access the solution?

By asking these questions, you move beyond surface-level thinking, deepen your understanding, and ultimately, position yourself and your team to make better, more informed decisions.

Let me share a story that illustrates the power of asking the right questions. During my time as a regional sales head, we faced a familiar challenge—losing market share to competitors. Instead of falling into the blame game between sales and marketing teams, we took a step back and focused on asking the right questions. Using organisational analysis templates familiar to all functions, we examined the problem holistically. This approach helped us avoid drawing partial or erroneous conclusions, much like the parable of blindfolded men touching different parts of an elephant and coming to vastly different interpretations. By staying focused on the problem, rather than on individuals or teams, we uncovered nuanced and complex root issues:

1. Distribution challenges (sales team's responsibility)
2. Brand equity issues (marketing team's responsibility)
3. Innovation launch support (joint responsibility)

This distributed responsibility and joint accountability defused emotions and fostered constructive, solution-oriented discussions. We called our turnaround plan *Palat* (Hindi for 'turnaround'), which led to significant improvements. Some actions even contributed to national-level success for certain brands.

The key takeaway here is that in stressful, hyper-competitive situations, proactively taking ownership of the end-to-end problem and asking the right questions can help you get ahead of challenges. It allows you to collaborate with colleagues rather than viewing them with suspicion. Remember, the power to ask questions isn't confined to any one person in an organisation; it's a privilege open to everyone. Once asked, the right questions take on a life of their own, persisting until real answers emerge, much like a game of whack-a-mole.

So, are you ready to unlock deeper insights by asking more thoughtful questions?

Ask the right questions at work.

So, What Do You Think?

'So, what do you think?' This is probably one of the most powerful questions a teammate or boss can ask you. It instantly signals respect, boosts your confidence by showing that your boss believes you belong in the role, and creates an opportunity to share your thoughts and make a lasting impression. But an important question here is: have you prepped enough to say something amazing when these five words are spoken? Have you done your homework? Are you working from a mindset that every time I am asked this, I am going to leave an indelible impression? Or do you fumble for an answer because you weren't expecting to be asked this question? Hence, it's important to be always ready with your answer. A day, time, and place will come when a good boss asks you this question, and the answer you give may change your life.

So, what do you think?

Make sure you are prepared to seize the opportunity when asked, 'So, what do you think?'

(This insight is inspired by one of the best bosses and individuals I have had the privilege of working with, who always asked this question.)

The Impact of Explaining the 'Why'

Every day, in my work, I see the benefits of explaining to folks why I am asking for something or why I said what I said in the meeting or email. For example, why I asked for a change in meeting time or why I am asking for something urgently. Explaining the 'why' behind small things during interactions with colleagues has proven crucial in getting things done, especially in a problem-solution context. The fact is that the small details and brief interactions matter. Those quick corridor chats can make a difference when you take the time to explain the reasoning behind your actions.

I remember this one exciting time in Kenya when we were working hard to grow our market share in toothpaste, where we were the challenger brand. A big gap in our market share was explained by not being present in the fast-growing herbal segment of the market. We used to import our toothpaste from Vietnam, and we were struggling to get our forecast accepted by the factory team in Vietnam owing to high-capacity utilisation. This was compounded by the difficulty in communication between our teams—language barriers, cultural barriers, time zone differences for organising enough meetings, differing priorities, and an overall feeling of being stuck.

As luck or a twist of fate would have it, my family and I were planning a holiday trip to Vietnam in the summer to visit old college friends who were based there. I thought to myself, why not try something unexpected? Why not visit the factory team there to say hello and see what happens! And yes, this did not land well with my family, and I am not sure I will try such a stunt again without thinking it through and planning it better first. So, I hesitantly reached out to the country supply chain and told him I was in the country and had heard great things about this factory (I had) and that I wanted to visit and learn how they did it. Surprisingly, he agreed and even sent me his car to visit the factory. The team at the factory was curious to see this person come all the way from Kenya to understand their work and were most gracious with their time and sharing their learnings. I energetically outlined the reality of the Kenyan business, painting our David versus Goliath battle as a challenger brand. With words laced with hope, I conveyed why their factory was crucial to our success and how grateful we would be for their support. They shared their challenges and innovative ideas. After one lunch and multiple coffees, we had the skeleton of a workable plan. Both teams thrashed out the details with determination, and within months, we excitedly launched in Kenya, taking the market by storm. All because of taking the time to explain why.

So, take that extra minute in your next request to add the why. It will help!

Take the time to explain why—it makes a difference.

The Art of Unpacking the Real Question

What is the question behind the question? The more I ask this in conversations and clarify it when I ask questions, the quicker and easier it becomes to reach the core of the discussion. Even in simple transactions, explaining the reason behind your question or request elicits a faster and better response from people, in my experience. For instance, if you are a super busy boss or manager, take the time to explain yourself. It will make a world of difference. And if you are in a discussion with others, ask the other person(s) what the question behind the question is. What is really on their mind? What is bothering them? What is their intent? What is the deeper point they want to raise? It will open a very different discussion and lead to very different outcomes.

I will conclude this section with an essential piece of advice for newcomers looking to fast-track their growth in the corporate world: master the art of reading between the lines. This isn't just a skill; it's a game-changer.

The next time you are in a conversation, try to peel back the layers. Is your colleague asking for a deadline extension because they are overwhelmed, or because they are unclear about the project's direction? Is your boss inquiring about your progress because they are genuinely concerned, or because they need material for their own presentation? Remember, everyone has motives, fears, and aspirations driving their actions. By tuning into these underlying currents, you are not just answering questions but also addressing real needs and building genuine connections. This is how you develop emotional intelligence and become the person who truly understands people, not just their words.

So, are you ready to become the office mind-reader? It's a superpower worth developing.

Clarifying the question behind the question leads to faster answers.

Why Are You Writing that Email?

In today's corporate landscape, we have all become email warriors. Let's dive into the murky waters of workplace email etiquette and uncover some truths to elevate your inbox game.

1. **The Email Dilemma: To Send or Not to Send?**

    Why are you really writing that email? Is it to:
    - Share vital information?
    - Document important decisions?
    - Clarify a complex issue?

    If you answered yes to any of these, congratulations! You are using email as intended. But if you are typing 'As we discussed . . .' just because you don't trust your colleague to remember the conversation, stop for a moment. That trust issue might be bigger than any email can solve.

2. **The CC Conundrum: Friend or Foe?**

    Now, let's talk about everyone's favourite email feature: the CC field. In this field, are you adding your boss because:
    - They need to be in the loop?
    - You are covering your bases?
    - You don't trust the recipient?

    If your answer isn't the first, you need to rethink. While CC'ing your boss might feel like a safety net, studies show it can actually make your colleagues feel less trusted and that's counterproductive.

3. **The Email Avoidance Dance**

    Are you using email to dodge awkward face-to-face conversations? Hate to break it to you, but that's not helping. Email is a fantastic tool, but it's no substitute for handling conflict or building trust. Sometimes, you have just got to bite the bullet and have that honest, in-person conversation.

4. **The Trust Factor: Building Bridges, Not Walls**
   At the heart of all this email chaos lies trust. If you are constantly documenting every conversation or CC'ing half the company, it's worth stepping back to address the underlying trust issues. A team that trusts one another is like a well-oiled machine—efficient, effective, and far less stressed about their inboxes.

So, before firing off that email or adding a crowd to the CC field, pause and ask yourself: 'Is this really necessary?' Your inbox (and your colleagues) will thank you.

So, why are you writing that email again?

Who Is the Chosen One?

Morpheus informed Neo in *The Matrix*: 'You are The One.' I wish it was that easy in real life! As projects and tasks become more complex and cross-functional in nature, it becomes much harder to figure out who is accountable for their success. And God forbid if things get delayed or fail, you will see the quick revival of your childhood game of 'passing the parcel'!

One simple thing I learnt from one of my bosses is that, apart from good network planning, assigning clear task-wise responsibilities, and doing regular pit stop checks, there's one task that the boss must do without fail, and that is clearly identifying the one person who is ultimately responsible for everything. Not two, not three—just one. But it's not as easy as it sounds. Think of the last project or task you led, which had multiple stakeholders and team members. Now, think if you could have held just one person accountable for it. This doesn't mean they do everything themselves—far from it. Instead, they become the central point of responsibility; the person who loses sleep if things go off track. They are the conductor of the orchestra, ensuring every instrument plays its part in perfect harmony.

So, the next time you are starting a project in this corporate matrix, ask yourself: 'Who's my Neo?'

Kick-start the project only after you have identified 'the one'.

Key Takeaways

- Ask more often: 'How you doin'?'
- Be (well) read and (very) ready.
- Keep an eye out for what is not there.
- 90% analysis + 10% solution = 100% results.
- Ask the right questions at work.
- Make sure you are prepared to seize the opportunity when asked, 'So, what do you think?'
- Take the time to explain why—it makes a difference.
- Clarifying the question behind the question leads to faster answers.
- So, why are you writing that email again?
- Kick-start the project only after you have identified 'the one'.

7
THE SECRET TO SUCCESSFUL TEAMWORK

Ever Tried Playing Football Without Goalposts?

Imagine two teams on the field, the ball in play, ready to go. The whistle blows, and the game begins. The ball is passed around, with teams trying to retain possession . . . but wait, there's no goalpost. What now? Just keep retaining possession and passing the ball? To what end? That is what happens when you start something without clear, measurable performance indicators. For example, when someone continues doing things simply because 'that's how it's always been done', without considering the link between input and output. Or when a team stays busy, constantly passing the ball, but nothing ever changes. Do these examples sound familiar? Therefore, it's pointless to keep passing the ball around when there's no goalpost to kick it into. So, stop what you are doing and set up the goalpost (understand the real problem, identify what will truly make a difference, establish the right input and output metrics), and then restart.

Set goalposts up first, then play to win.

My Idea or Yours?

More and more, I am seeing that when diverse individuals and teams collaborate, the best outcomes don't come from simply selecting the top idea from each person or sub-team. Instead, they emerge from creating a new idea—a synthesis of different parts of the ideas contributed by individuals and sub-teams. In simple terms, it's not just your idea or mine, but a new idea formed from that holds the greatest potential. The tricky part? Creating the conditions for this to happen. Meaning, that if the organisational culture celebrates individual stars, it's probably harder to achieve this because it boils down to my survival versus yours. If reward structures lean heavily toward individual differentiation rather than team output, it becomes tougher since it's about my chance to earn more than you. On the other hand, if the culture prioritises team and organisational goals as critical, if the organisation has a purpose that acts as a North Star attracting individuals who align with it, and if leaders lead by example, then the probability of the 'wisdom of crowds' delivering amazing outcomes increases significantly.

Here's an example of when I pushed forward with what I thought was a brilliant idea, only to see it fail so spectacularly and quickly that I was left stunned. It was a brand extension idea for a skincare product we sold in Africa. In skincare, extending a brand across adjacent product formats is common, so the concept had merit. Additionally, the brand was strong in its existing category, making it seem logical to expand into a related one. So, we did. A logical business case, a good product, solid pricing, and a capable cross-functional team all geared up for the launch. And then . . . nothing. No traction and no sales. Ouch. I wanted to bury my head in the sand like an ostrich and pretend it never happened.

Why did it fail? Because I had put so many positive filters on my thinking, focusing on reasons the idea would succeed, I neglected to consider the reasons it might fail. I didn't ask the team to challenge the idea. I didn't seek wider opinions. Simply put, I chose my idea over engaging the group in deciding what to do. If I had involved the team, I would have learnt about blind spots I missed, like the competition having a better product at a much lower price, with superior distribution and awareness. We had no compelling reasons for consumers to switch.

This experience taught me the true value of the wisdom of crowds, the power of humility, the importance of being open-minded, and the necessity of respecting others' views.

My idea + Your idea = Better idea.

(Inspired in part from the book *Wisdom of Crowds* by James Surowiecki)

Personal Touch: Customising Messages to Increase Responses

One morning, I sent an email starting with 'Dear All' and got zero responses. On another occasion, I sent an email starting with 'Dear [Individual]' and received loads of responses! This got me thinking. The key difference between these two approaches was that the first involved mass communication with no personalisation, while the second was a tailored, individualised approach, resulting in a significant increase in engagement. It was then that I realised the power of simple reciprocity. If someone extends their hand near you, your hand instinctively goes out for a handshake. Similarly, when you feel someone is reaching out to you personally, it resonates, and you naturally want to respond.

But it's not easy. Writing to everyone is simpler; it's like a broadcast sent out at large. Crafting a personal message is tougher. It requires effort to narrow down, get specific, and think about the individual you are addressing. It demands clarity in what you want, who you want it from, and why. It is the 90-10 rule in action again—spend 90 per cent of your time thinking carefully about your purpose, your audience, and your ask, and then act with precision.

Reach out to individuals individually.

The Value of Genuine One-on-One Connections

In my experience, one-on-one interactions work best—not team outings, virtual coffee catch-ups, or social drinks evenings, but genuine one-on-one connections. It significantly reduces unnecessary tension and stress while greatly building trust and teamwork. Thus, taking the time to build those connections and relationships goes a long way in addressing the things that never get said in big formal meetings.

As a young sales manager, I faced a major challenge when our company merged two category sales teams. Each category had its own dedicated team and area managers, and the merger aimed to drive synergies and economies of scale. While no jobs were cut, the success of the merger depended on seamless teamwork, including the transfer of knowledge and team members. Our new boss, soon to lead both teams, did something incredibly smart. The day before the merger, he gathered all the sales managers and told us to clear our schedules and arrive early the next morning. That night, curiosity ran high.

The next morning, we nervously assembled, feeling like it was the first day of college. Event organisers split us into pairs with colleagues we barely knew and handed us a slip of paper. It was a city-wide treasure hunt! Each clue led us to a new location, requiring close collaboration. The goal was clear: spend the day getting to know each other without it ever being explicitly stated. By sunset, the final clue brought us to a seaside resort, where our boss was waiting with a projector on the beach. Instead of a formal briefing, he handed out popcorn, and we watched *Apollo 13*, a movie about teamwork in the face of adversity. Afterwards, we shared our experiences and realised we had learnt more about each other that day than any formal session could have taught us. That bonding created an indomitable team spirit that stayed with us beyond our roles at the time. Thanks to this human-centric approach, we executed the change plan flawlessly.

So, take the time to connect with your teammates outside of meetings. It truly makes a difference.

Give that person you have only been emailing a call and grab a cuppa together.

Parking Lot, Storage Box, and Conflict Resolution

The solution to meeting conflicts lies in a parking lot and a storage box. Let me explain.

Meetings often turn into battlegrounds over conflicting ideas. In my experience, great teams handle this by first side-stepping the areas of conflict to find areas of consensus. This is a masterclass in setting aside ego and immaturity. Then come the conflict areas. I have seen great teams segment these areas of disagreement into two distinct categories: a parking lot and a storage box.

1. The parking lot is for urgent, high-conflict topics that need immediate attention and resolution. Like a real parking lot, it's a temporary space that incurs a cost.
2. The storage box is for less critical, contentious topics— those that may or may not be important but aren't urgent and can wait without causing harm.

Thus, whenever a conflict arises, segmenting the issues correctly helps the team prioritise effectively, starting with the costly parking lot items before moving on to the others. Disastrous teams (if you can even call them teams) fail to clear the first hurdle, i.e., side-stepping conflicts to find areas of consensus. For such teams, the solution lies in going back to basics and checking for trust alignment. Then there are teams that manage the first step but falter in the second. These not-so-great teams misallocate issues to the wrong categories: minor issues take up valuable time in the parking lot, while significant conflicts are sidelined in the storage box. Sorting this out requires setting aside egos, believing in the collective wisdom of the group, and having the humility to accept that even if things go wrong, the group did its best.

The next time you are in a meeting with conflicts, take the time to carefully determine what belongs in the parking lot and what goes in the storage box. This small tweak might be just what your team needs to make effective, efficient decisions with real impact.

The parking lot and storage box approach can be effective in resolving conflicts.

Difficult Situation or Difficult People?

Reflecting on difficult situations I have encountered, I have realised that some were inherently difficult, while others were made difficult by the people involved. Understanding the nature of the challenge—whether it's the situation itself or the people—can help navigate it effectively. However, in the heat of the moment, it's easy to confuse the two, which can lead to missteps. Here are some observations that can help you better navigate such scenarios.

If it's a difficult situation, shared acknowledgement helps. Stating that the situation is challenging—not the people—

can shift the focus toward collaboration. Adjustments, the combined wisdom of diverse opinions, and empathy for the bigger picture can help everyone move toward a solution. However, if the issue lies with difficult people, navigating it becomes much tougher. In both corporate and personal life, you sometimes have the option to walk away, though not without consequences. When walking away isn't an option, you have to work through it with fortitude, frustration, and the understanding that it will demand mental perseverance.

This reflection is tricky because it's subjective and could lead to a 'victim' mindset, where the blame is placed entirely on others. So why discuss it? Because over time, I have learnt to discern whether the difficulty stems from myself, the situation, or the people involved. When the difficulty arises from differences in opinions or objectives, dialogue can often resolve it. If the differences are fundamental, a resolution might not be possible, and that is okay. But when people consistently fail to follow through on commitments, contradict themselves, or shift blame onto others, that is where I draw the line. Navigating such dynamics requires caution and deliberate action.

Reflecting on a particularly trying experience, I recall working with a distributor partner who seemed intent on obstructing progress. Every collaborative effort met resistance, accompanied by excuses undermining our ideas, distribution strategies, and pricing. Despite our genuine attempts to understand their operations, we were met with vague reassurances to 'just trust us'. The frustration only grew as the distributor bypassed us to escalate complaints directly to our superiors. Eventually, it became clear that we were at an impasse, working with someone whose beliefs and objectives were irreconcilable with ours. Parting ways, though messy, was the only viable solution.

This experience taught me a sobering truth: sometimes, no matter how much effort you invest, you can't bridge the gap with someone determined to be difficult. In such cases, it's the obstinacy of the individual that becomes the greatest barrier to progress.

Assess whether you are dealing with a challenging situation or difficult individuals, and then tailor your solution accordingly.

Is That Meeting Necessary?

Are you thinking about calling a meeting? Hold that thought. There are only three solid reasons to gather everyone in a conference room:

1. **Decision-Making Pow-Wows**

   When it's crunch time for decisions, who is incharge? Here's what works: Focus on the situation, not who is at the top of the hierarchy. Give more weight to those bearing the risk and those willing to own the outcome, even if it flops. It is like a game of responsibility hot potato.

2. **Open Innovation Brainstorms**

   Want to supercharge your team? Encourage them to tap into the 'wisdom of crowds'. This isn't just feel-good stuff; it's practical. Group wisdom lowers risks, boosts ownership, and points you in the right direction.

3. **Info-Exchange Sessions**

   Traditional update meetings? Ditch them. A concise, one-page memo does the trick. But for the juicy, off-the-record kind of stuff that wouldn't make it into a formal note, that is where meetings shine.

So, next time you are about to hit 'schedule meeting', ask yourself: decision, innovation, or information? If it's not one of these, maybe reconsider sending that invite.

Essentials of a good meeting: decision, innovation, and information.

Decoding Meeting Dynamics

If you have attended enough meetings, you have likely noticed how some colleagues arrive meticulously prepared with color-coded notes, while others seem to be piecing their thoughts together mid-sentence. Welcome to the fascinating world of meeting dynamics, where understanding and decoding different thinking styles can become your secret weapon for success. Here are some of the most prominent thinking styles you will encounter:

1. **Pre-thinkers**

   These individuals think before they speak. They are the ones who have read the agenda, gone through the pre-read materials, reflected on the topic, scribbled notes, and highlighted key points in their diaries or printouts. When they share their thoughts, they are well-considered and deliberate. Take their views seriously, as they rely on good old-fashioned hard work to get their points across. To engage effectively, you will need the stamina and speed to keep up with their thorough preparation and determined approach.

2. **Mid-thinkers**

    These are the people who think while they are speaking. You will recognise them by the 'errs', 'umms', and frequent pauses as they refine their thoughts in real-time. They might backtrack, reframe, or restart their sentences, which can make their delivery seem scattered. However, don't dismiss their opinions—they are brave enough to think on their feet and confident in their ability to adapt. To work effectively with them, stay sharp and ready to engage dynamically.

3. **Post-thinkers**

    These individuals process their thoughts after speaking. While rare, this happens when people cling to repeating the same beliefs, rely heavily on past successes, or hold pre-formed views that resist new information. Making progress with post-thinkers is challenging, as their entrenched perspectives can act as a roadblock. To navigate this, you will need to be at your most creative and persuasive to encourage them to consider alternate viewpoints.

So, next time you are in a meeting, watch out for these thinking styles. And remember that it's not just about what is said, but how and when the thinking happens that can guide your next moves.

Recognising different thinking styles will help you engage more effectively and guide you in making your next moves.

Resources: The Usual and the Unusual

For any team project, we typically consider capital, labour, and skills as key resources. When it comes to labour or people, our perspective has evolved over time—from ensuring we have enough people to focusing on whether they possess the right capabilities, and now, to also evaluating if they have the appropriate level of confidence and capacity. This is the 'usual'. So, the question arises then what is the 'unusual'?

Consider trust as an unseen yet omnipresent resource that is arguably the most critical for a team project to succeed. Trust is built on past experiences, mutual respect, shared goals, and similar factors. It forms the foundational resource that often goes unacknowledged.

So, the next time you start a project, assess how much trust exists within the team and how you can increase it. Building trust involves navigating team performance stages (forming, storming, norming, performing), fostering psychological safety, and aligning goals. Strengthening this invisible resource might just make the difference between success and failure.

Resources = Capital + Labour +Skills + Trust.

Doveryai, No Proveryai (Trust, but Verify)

Trust is the bedrock of effective teamwork, but as the Russian proverb goes, 'Trust, but verify'. This principle, popularised by Reagan and Gorbachev, is particularly crucial in the corporate world. Let's explore why this matters and how it can save you when the stakes are high.

1. **The Ideal Versus Reality**

   In a perfect world, trust—built on experience, skills, past results, intent, and shared vision—would suffice. But we don't live in a perfect world, do we? As any good engineer knows, nothing operates flawlessly. That's why we have safeguards, fail-safes, and monitoring systems in factories and machines.

2. **Trust, but Verify in Action**

   Think of your work as a daily Sudoku puzzle. You rely on others, and they rely on you. Objectives can clash, ideas may misalign, and assumptions often shift. It's a miracle anything gets done! This is where 'trust, but verify' becomes your secret weapon. Let me share a story that cemented this lesson for me.

   One day, I was called into an urgent meeting. My brand manager and supply chain team looked like they had seen a ghost. The crisis? We were running out of jars for our bestseller. Relying on a single supplier (mistake number one), maintaining a lean inventory (mistake number two), soaring demand, and failing moulds—a perfect storm in the making. We had a plan, sure, but our supplier was more confident than competent. Makeshift repairs failed and import documentation errors left us high and dry. We scrambled, sourcing jars from other markets at high costs and with delays. Just when we thought we had weathered the storm, another crisis struck: more moulds failing, imported ones still stuck. I had just assured my bosses the crisis was over. Talk about egg on your face! This was when the penny dropped for me:

- Trust is king, but verification is queen.
- Trust the intent, verify the assumptions.
- Trust the competence, verify the confidence.
- Trust the system, verify its vitals.

In the end, we ended up micro-managing the supplier, redesigning their workflow, and implementing a rigorous verification process. It was a tough lesson, but one that stuck.

3. **Applying 'Trust, but Verify'**

    We have explored the importance of the 'trust, but verify' approach in the workplace. Now, let's dive into how you can apply this mindset to your own work.

    - Don't assume everything is fine just because someone says it is.
    - Implement regular check-ins and progress reports.
    - Create systems for easy verification without micromanagement.
    - Foster an environment where asking questions and seeking clarification is encouraged.

Overall 'trust, but verify' isn't about doubting intentions; it's about acknowledging that new and evolving situations bring complexities, and perfection is rare. Remember tust is the foundation of effective teamwork, but verification acts as your safeguard against unexpected setbacks. By balancing trust with a healthy dose of due diligence, you build stronger relationships while protecting yourself from unpleasant surprises.

So, trust your team, suppliers, and systems but always verify. Your future self will thank you.

Doveryrai, no proveryai (trust, but verify).

Key Takeaways

- Set goalposts up first, then play to win.
- My idea + Your idea = Better idea.
- Reach out to individuals individually.
- Give that person you have only been emailing a call and grab a cuppa together.
- The parking lot and storage box approach can be effective in resolving conflicts.
- Assess whether you are dealing with a challenging situation or difficult individuals, and then tailor your solution accordingly.
- Essentials of a good meeting: decision, innovation, and information.
- Recognising different thinking styles will help you engage more effectively and guide you in making your next moves.
- Resources = Capital + Labour + Skills + Trust.
- Doveryrai, no proveryai (trust, but verify).

8
NAVIGATING THE WORKPLACE CULTURE

Baby See, Baby Do

Parents know this better than anyone: kids imitate and adopt their parents' behaviours. Interestingly, the same holds true in workplaces, even among adults! New employees observe seasoned colleagues to understand how to fit in, while all employees take cues from their bosses on how to operate and behave. The work culture is so heavily top-driven that it's surprising it isn't more widely recognised as the primary tool for driving organisational change. The saying 'Be the change you want to see' is something we have all heard, and it holds true here.

If you want to change the culture or behaviour of your team, start by changing your own. Act the way you want your team to act, use the language you want them to use, and consistently walk the talk. You will begin to see shifts almost immediately—no need to wait for an expensive cultural change expert to teach the team what to do.

What you do is what your team will do.

Be a Radiator, Not a Vacuum Cleaner

Certain people radiate warmth and positive energy. They set the right mood, tone, and environment, making everyone feel safe and engaged. As a result, things move forward, and tasks get done. On the flip side, some people exude cold vibes that drain the energy from a room. They create an atmosphere of unease, making others defensive. In such environments, progress stalls, and nothing seems to get accomplished. A related point is the often-undervalued skill of being easy to work with. People naturally gravitate toward collaborating with those who are approachable, constructive, and dependable. Conversely, there are those who are difficult to work with—be it due to negativity, lack of reliability, or poor communication—making teamwork unnecessarily challenging and less enjoyable.

When reflecting on workplace culture, I have realised it always starts with me. I always ask myself whether I am radiating positivity and hope, or whether I am draining energy and instilling fear. During my best stints, I was a radiator; in my less-than-great periods, I have also become a vacuum cleaner. If I could go back, this is one behaviour I would work to change.

I recall a particularly challenging sales stint when things weren't going well. In desperation, I started calling senior team members on Saturdays, one-on-one, to figure out what was going wrong and what needed to be done. Looking back, this was a low point. First, I was reaching out to people who didn't report to me directly, effectively bypassing their bosses—yikes! It is cringeworthy to even write about now. Perhaps it stemmed from a lack of trust, maturity in managing big teams, or my inability to handle pressure. But there I was, hot-headed, pacing around my bedroom, upsetting my family, scribbling notes on their commitments, and chasing progress throughout the week. Then, I would call them again the next Saturday to check in. And so, the cycle continued.

Did this approach yield short-term results? Yes. Did it cause medium-term chaos? Absolutely. Was I able to turn things around in the long term? Thankfully, yes. Eventually, I recognised the flaws in my approach and stopped. However, the damage—to my health, relationships, and morale—had been done. My constant self-imposed stress and confusion about accountability with responsibility fuelled this destructive behaviour. The turning point came when my team shared candid feedback about my leadership style. We established mutual agreements on how to work together, supported one another's success, celebrated achievements, shared learnings, and grew through collective experiences. In short, I started off as a vacuum cleaner but thankfully ended up as a radiator.

Strive to be the best version of yourself—someone positive, constructive, and easy to work with.

Be like a radiator—spread warmth and positive energy.

Agreeing and Disagreeing the Right Way

Be gracious when complimenting and be graceful when disagreeing. I have seen and learnt from the very best how these qualities go a long way in fostering better collaboration and getting things done. I have also been in countless meetings where negative emotions and egos join forces to create havoc. Insults replace ideas, and by the end, nothing meaningful is achieved. On the other hand, when people are gracious, it fosters positive emotions and lowers ego defences. When people are graceful, it builds dignity and mutual respect. Together, these qualities help overcome challenges and lead to meaningful outcomes.

So, if you want results, remember this: building a great culture is rooted in mutual respect, and a key part of that is how we agree and disagree.

Whether you are offering a compliment or expressing disagreement, do it the right way.

Imposters Beware

Three golden rules I have learnt over time for fostering a thriving organisational culture are as follows:

1. **Do not tolerate imposters**
   - Call out BS when you see it.
   - Create a culture where people don't need to pretend.
2. **Do not have imposter syndrome**
   - You deserve to be here.
   - You are smarter than you think.

3. **Do not be an imposter**
   - It is okay not to know everything, even if you belong.
   - Focus on continuously learning and contributing.

I have had my own ups and downs in this space. Early in my career, I struggled with imposter syndrome. I felt like I didn't truly fit in for almost a decade. It wasn't until my stint in Africa that I felt truly settled. Here's what helped, and I hope it resonates with anyone navigating similar challenges:

1. **Fresh Starts Matter**

   The opportunity for a clean slate, where no one knew me, was transformative. Fresh starts may seem rare, but I have learnt they can happen anytime. A new boss, evolving job challenges, or even peer feedback sessions can create a reset. Embracing this mindset was a game-changer for me.

2. **Support Networks Are Invaluable**

   At a time when I doubted my technical skills, a close friend nudged me to read *How Brands Grow* by Byron Sharp. That book not only boosted my knowledge but validated my way of thinking. Friends, family, mentors, and coaches can provide the right nudge at the right time.

3. **Playful Curiosity Helps**

   I threw myself into my role with curiosity—asking questions, gaining hands-on experience, travelling, and reading. Each day became a building block for learning, which, in turn, made me the go-to person on the job. That trust reinforced my confidence and capabilities.

Even now, I am not always successful at following these principles, and it still troubles me. Every missed opportunity creates a small crack for imposter syndrome to sneak through. Yet, this challenge keeps me striving to stay on my A-game. It is a double-edged sword—sometimes it cuts me, and sometimes I cut through it. And so the journey continues!

Don't tolerate an imposter. Don't have imposter syndrome. Don't be an imposter.

The Safety Net of Support

I fondly remember my first sales stint. Most of the sales team members in the region were nearly double my age and much more worldly-wise than I was. It was during this stint that, unfortunately, I lost my father to a fatal heart attack. It was unexpected and happened while I was visiting my parents over a weekend break from work. The shock of what happened took away my composure. This occurred late in the evening, and much later that night, I managed to message my boss about it.

Early the next morning, I found the local sales team manager and his team, who were based in the city, at my doorstep. They immediately took charge of the situation. They helped in every way throughout the day, from figuring out funeral arrangements to arranging food for family members who came after hearing the news, to just being there for me to lean on. I will never forget that day. Ever.

Later, my team called and took charge of all work-related matters for a long time as I found my way back from grief to work. It took me a while, and the way my boss and my team rallied around me reflected the reality of the organisation I worked for. Caring was, and still is, its DNA.

It is in tough situations like these that you know if you are working in a good place—a place as supportive as a safety net, where everyone looks out for everyone else. If you find yourself in a place like this, thrive in it. If you find yourself in a place that is not like this, do right by caring for others yourself, and hopefully watch them pay it forward. Otherwise, maybe it's time to make exit plans.

Here's musing that shows what a truly supportive workplace looks like:

You help others more because others are helping you.

You take a break when you need to, without worry, because someone has got your back, and you know you will have someone else's back when the time comes.

You share your knowledge because you know someone else will share theirs with you.

You share credit for the output with everyone, as everyone else is sharing credit for the output with you.

You feel happy working together and achieving more than you could individually.

You feel safe.

You worry less.

You achieve more.

We all achieve more.

Tomorrow gets better when we all care for one another today.

What Needs to Happen Versus What Ends Up Happening

Ever been in a meeting where it felt like everyone was dancing around the real issues? Let's break it down:

1. **What should happen:**
   - You speak the hard truths.
   - Others hear the real challenges.
2. **What often happens:**
   - You sugarcoat things to look good.
   - Others hear that everything's fine.

Here's the thing: magic happens when these four align. That's when we face the brutal facts, have honest talks, explore different ideas, and make smart choices. But how do we get there? It's all about creating a culture where people feel safe to speak up. And that starts with leaders who encourage honesty and openness. Remember, great meetings aren't about making things sound good; they are about making things good.

Culture of candour = What needs to be said and heard is indeed what is said and heard.

Decision-Making in the Boardroom: What Makes It Work

Have you ever wondered why some corporate boardroom decisions get executed well while others do not? My top reasons, based on my experience are as follows:

1. **Culture of Candour**

   The ability of the team to stand up and say when something won't work, when a certain assumption is wrong, or simply to have a frank discussion on the pros and cons of a decision is at the top of my list.

2. **Trust**

   Trust in each other, based on mutual trust in intent and competence, is the next crucial factor. This is the foundation on which all decisions are truly built. If this is wobbly, things will start toppling almost as soon as folks walk out of that real or virtual boardroom.

3. **Wisdom of Crowds**

   A brilliant concept, outlined by James Surowiecki in his book, emphasises the importance of team thinking and working towards solutions that build on each other's ideas and the power of collective intelligence.

So, before diving into analysis and decision-making, ensure these elements are in place, and then watch the magic unfold. Let me share a story from my time in Kenya that illustrates the same.

Chombo hakiendi ikiwa kila mtu anapiga makasia yake is a Swahili proverb that translates to 'A boat doesn't move forward if everyone rows in their own direction.' It perfectly captures the delicate balance between individual effort and teamwork. At one point, I was convinced that my local knowledge gave me a better understanding of consumer needs than my colleagues in Singapore and London. Spoiler alert: I was wrong. The products I launched based on local insights flopped spectacularly. While I understood the local realities, I missed crucial brand dynamics and consumer behaviour nuances. On the other hand, the global team knew their brands inside out but struggled with local subtleties. Their solo efforts also failed.

After these setbacks, we changed our approach. Instead of engaging in a competitive tug-of-war over who knew best, we united. We trusted each other to handle different aspects of the challenge and shared accountability. The result? Stunning success.

This experience turned me into a staunch advocate for the 'wisdom of crowds' in the workplace. Working constructively with others—complementing rather than competing—is the secret sauce to impactful achievements. And yes, I have learnt to capitalise on moments of challenge. That's when teams come together out of sheer necessity!

Remember, it's not just about you versus others; it's about you and others. As The Beatles wisely said that we need to come together. So, next time you are in that boardroom, ask yourself: Are we rowing in the same direction? Are we leveraging our collective wisdom? The answers to these questions could be the difference between a decision that sinks and one that soars.

Candour + Trust + Wisdom of crowds = Execution excellence.

Hope as a Catalyst for Culture and Success

Starting out in the corporate world can sometimes feel overwhelming, especially when the environment seems tough, and challenges appear insurmountable. But here's something to hold on to: hope. Hope isn't just a feel-good concept; it's a powerful force that can shape your career, your team, and the culture around you. Build hope within yourself and spread it to those around you. The culture you want to be part of will naturally grow from this foundation. You can spark hope by being fair, honest, trustworthy, and by creating a safe environment where people feel valued. These small actions can ignite a chain reaction, inspiring others to do more, achieve more, and hope for more.

Looking back on my own career, I have realised that my best work has always come when I felt hopeful and energised. On the other hand, hopelessness leads to stagnation. Being known as someone who inspires hope is one of the most valuable personal brands you can build. It makes people want to work with you and trust you. Here's how you can start cultivating hope in your workplace:

1. **Celebrate Small Wins**

    Progress fuels momentum, making every step forward meaningful.

2. **Set Realistic Goals**

    Achievable targets build confidence and pave the way for greater success.

3. **Share Positivity**

    Uplifting stories inspire and energise those around you.

4. **Model Optimism**

    Your positive attitude is infectious and can transform the environment.

5. **Acknowledge Tough Times**

   It's okay to feel helpless; recognise those emotions, but channel them into seeking solutions and support.

Remember, hope isn't about ignoring challenges; it's about believing in your ability—and your team's ability—to overcome them. So, bring it to the table every day, and you will not only grow but also inspire those around you to grow with you.

Keep the flame of hope burning within you and strive to ignite hope in others.

Empowering Teams: Align, Trust, Succeed

Our ancestors survived by making smart choices that ultimately led to you and me being here today. The underlying foundation of these smart choices was having the freedom to make the choices in the first place. So, if there's no freedom, no choice then there's no evolution, no you and me.

Cut to today's corporate world, it's the same. Deep down, we like the freedom to choose as it seemingly gives us better control over our destiny. Anything that infringes on this choice is bound to cause friction, some minor and some major. Ergo, the much-ignored culture hack in my experience is empowering employees—giving power to the people. Trusting your team to do what's right. Folks like to be given responsibility and to be brought into confidence that you are indeed trusting them with something big and important. It makes all the difference. If you are the boss, try doing this and see the difference. If you are an individual contributor in a team, try raising your hand and asking for more responsibility and see the difference it makes.

In the heart of East Africa, amidst the vibrant rhythms of the land, I found myself tasked with orchestrating a marketing workshop on the theme of 'New Power' which was a celebration of the shifting tides, where consumers and influencers reign supreme, propelled by the winds of the internet and the rise of social media. This was a big event for me to lead and organise, and the stakes were high for me personally to land this successfully as a key deliverable of the year. No pressure! Instinctively, I felt the need to micromanage, given the high stakes and a belief that I had thought through the plan well. But fate intervened, whisking me away to an advertising festival, leaving me no choice but to entrust the vision to the capable hands of my team. And what they did by the time I returned, just in time for the workshop, blew my mind. For starters, they brought collective wisdom and imagination to the event with a local nuance I could never have done. They used their understanding of consumers and the ecosystem to design the event to be fit-for-purpose and loads of fun. Knowing it would make a difference to their own work; they went all out to prove they were amazing.

The lesson learnt was profound, etched in the very fabric of our success: the AA rule—align on outcomes, grant autonomy, and watch brilliance unfold. In the crucible of high stakes, true leadership is not found in dictation, but in empowerment. And in the symphony of collaboration, the sweetest melodies are those of trust and autonomy.

Empowered employees = Engage culture.

In the End, What Will We Remember?

The targets or the way we achieved them.

The everyday work or the one big thing we achieved.

The formal meetings or the informal get-togethers.

The average days or the days when something dramatic happened.

The boring chats or the debates that led to something amazing.

Long after we forget the numbers and targets, what will stay with us are:

The people we worked with,

The amazing moments, both surprising and shocking,

The emotions, both happy and sad, and

The stories, both believable and unbelievable.

Are you doing something today that you will remember tomorrow?

Key Takeaways

- What you do is what your team will do.
- Be like a radiator—spread warmth and positive energy.
- Whether you are offering a compliment or expressing disagreement, do it the right way.
- Don't tolerate an imposter. Don't have imposter syndrome. Don't be an imposter.
- Tomorrow gets better when we all care for one another today.
- Culture of candour = What needs to be said and heard is indeed what is said and heard.
- Candour + Trust + Wisdom of crowds = Execution excellence.
- Keep the flame of hope burning within you and strive to ignite hope in others.
- Empowered employees = Engage culture.
- Are you doing something today that you will remember tomorrow?

Part III
The Future You

'Education never ends, Watson. It is a series of lessons, with the greatest for the last.'
—Sherlock Holmes

When my thrilling time in Kenya came to an end, I felt a mix of contentment and restlessness. I craved more yet doubted my qualifications. This set the stage for a pivotal moment in my career, one that many of us encounter: the desire for growth coupled with self-doubt. It's a relatable starting point for discussing career advancement and personal development.

While pondering my next move, I stumbled upon an intriguing job listing on our company's internal portal. It was a hybrid strategy and chief-of-staff role, reporting to the global chief digital and commercial officer. Up until that point, my career had been rooted in intense market operations, with a focus on sales and marketing. I had often been seen as strategically inclined, and here was this role, seemingly tailor-made for my aspirations, appearing at the perfect moment.

Applying for this hybrid strategy and chief-of-staff role taught me a crucial lesson: sometimes, you need to take a leap of faith in your career. Despite my credentials not perfectly matching the job description, I decided to go all-in, crafting a compelling 'why hire me' presentation. This bold move paid off, leading to an unexpected interview and ultimately landing the job. This experience reinforced an important truth that to become the future version of yourself, you must commit wholeheartedly. Remember that outstanding opportunities aren't handed out and you need to actively pursue them.

I have distilled this lesson into a simple formula:

1. Working + Asking = Success.
2. Working + Not asking = Sadness.

3. Not working + Asking = Shocking.
4. Not working + Not asking = Slumber.

This formula underscores the importance of both effort and initiative in advancing your career.

Part III of the book builds on this personal anecdote to provide a practical guide on seizing opportunities and building upon them. It covers key aspects of career development:

1. **Getting Promoted**

    Practical lessons from experience and observation, applicable to both first-time and seasoned professionals seeking advancement.

2. **Becoming a First-Time Boss**

    Insights into a role that's rarely taught—formally or informally—based on my experiences working with twelve bosses and leading diverse teams.

3. **Transforming from Boss to Leader**

    The essential skills that elevate a boss into a true leader which entails gaining followers and embodying organisational values.

4. **What Really Matters**

    Understanding how to build your career while recognising factors beyond your control and emphasising the importance of resilience.

This section bridges the gap between where you are now and where you aspire to be. It's about taking charge of your professional growth, mastering the nuances of leadership, and maintaining perspective on what truly matters in the long run. By sharing personal experiences and practical advice, this part of the book will offer a roadmap for navigating your career journey and encourage readers to seize opportunities, embrace challenges, and continuously evolve into the future version of themselves.

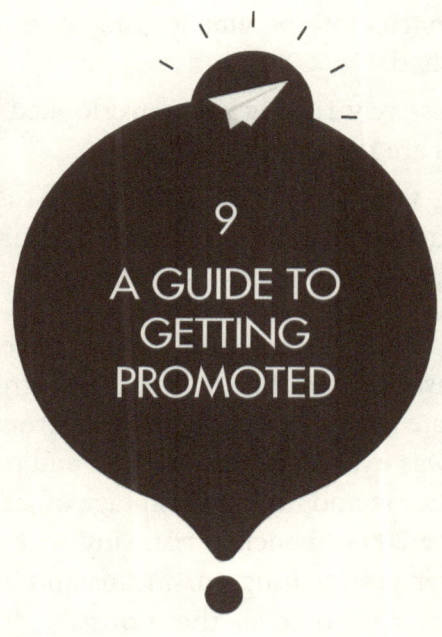

9
A GUIDE TO GETTING PROMOTED

Defining Success on Your Own Terms

If we want a promotion, we need to desire it, work for it, and ask for it. But what happens when you cross these hurdles and still don't get what you want? This is where many people stumble. The confidence built from overcoming obstacles often creates a confirmation bias that success is guaranteed. Yet sometimes, luck isn't on your side, you are in the wrong place at the wrong time, or someone else simply does everything you did but better. In such scenarios, there are typically three responses:

1. Quitting in frustration, often leading to impulsive choices later regretted.
2. Waiting passively, risking being overlooked when external candidates are favoured.
3. Evaluating what happened, dusting off disappointment, coming back stronger by improving yourself and your impact, and assessing options thoughtfully yet decisively.

The third approach is the most constructive, helping you accept the consequences of your choices and grow from them. Let me illustrate this with a personal story from my career.

In 2010, I was expecting a promotion and pay rise. Riding on this expectation and taking advantage of falling real estate prices post the 2008 financial crisis, my wife and I decided to buy a property, stretching our means and banking on the anticipated pay rise to cover the mortgage. Then came the gut punch: my boss informed me that the promotion wasn't happening immediately. Instead, the offer on the table was to switch to another role at a higher level, contingent on availability and someone being willing to take me on. Faced with this challenge, three things happened:

1. I found a new role, with the promotion dependent on my performance in the first six months. I poured every ounce of energy into proving myself, learning invaluable lessons about going above and beyond.
2. A frank discussion with my wife led to collaborative financial management, including downsizing our living arrangements to ease the burden.
3. This challenging period ultimately led to my dream job, showing that sometimes, adversity paves the way for opportunity.

This experience taught me that when faced with career setbacks, the most constructive approach is to evaluate, adapt, and persevere. By choosing to improve myself, reassess my options, and make thoughtful decisions, I not only overcame the immediate challenge but also positioned myself for greater opportunities. It reinforced that the path to career growth isn't always linear and that how we respond to setbacks can often be more important than the setbacks themselves.

PS: A great TED Talk related to this topic is by Valerie Kondos Field, titled *Why Winning Doesn't Always Equal Success*. She emphasises the importance of being champions in life and not just in competitions.

Sometimes things don't go as planned, but what truly matters is how you approach, respond to, and move forward from the situation.

Acing the Two Ps for Career Success

When it comes to promotions, we often hear about the two dreaded P words: performance and potential. If you have got these two Ps under your belt, you are on your way up—or so the boss says! Based on my experience, here's a simple insight into these two Ps:

1. **On Performance**

    While acing all your KPIs is important, having one big success story under your belt usually makes a significant difference. This is especially crucial because it's often the boss's boss who decides on your promotion, and a standout success story helps you become more than just another name on the list.

2. On Potential

Beyond everything else, it's about operating at an N+1 level. This means thinking and acting like the person whose job you are aiming for. It is not just about fulfilling your current responsibilities; it's about demonstrating that you are ready for the next level.

Performance + Potential = Promotion.

Go 1 UP

You might think you are ready to take on the part of the boss's job that you see, and for very valid reasons. But what about the tasks they handle that you have no clue about because you are not part of those conversations? Do you learn those when you take the job, or is there a better way?

To understand everything your boss does, start by requesting to be part of forums where your boss typically represents your team. Ask to attend meetings where they discuss key matters with their boss and seek opportunities to be included in higher-level work to learn and develop yourself. Additionally, offer to take over your boss's responsibilities when they are on leave. Know that doing your current role well doesn't guarantee you will excel at the next level, as it's a different job in scale, scope, and expectation. Hence, you need to go 1UP if you want to set yourself up for success.

Early on in my career, I rarely went 1UP. I was either scared, clueless, unsure, or a mix of all these! In hindsight, I can see the signs: my colleagues would step up or be asked to step up when the boss wasn't around, and over time, those who took that opportunity to showcase their potential did well. When I spoke to a few of them later in life, the straightforward realisation for me was that all of them were scared, clueless, or unsure in those moments, but they went ahead anyway—they took the leap of faith. That was the difference. My honest advice to myself after that was to always put my hand up as fast as I possibly could to do more and learn more when it came to going 1UP. And boy, did it help.

Going 1UP works when you are confident it will help you learn more and take you toward your goals. It is like moving 'from' to 'to':

- From 'What is my job?' to 'What is the problem?'
- From 'I am waiting to be told what to do' to 'What can I start doing now?'
- From 'I don't want to fail' to 'I want to succeed.'
- From 'I am not clear on my goals' to 'I will start by setting goals on my own.'

Let me share a recent professional milestone. In my role as a strategy lead and chief of staff, I got one of my best performance appraisals for keeping the team together after my then-boss moved on. I had no boss for six months, and I took it upon myself to keep the team focused on key work objectives. Personally, I raised my hand for more work and helped other teams with their tasks where my skills could be put to good use. A team working on a high-profile, critical project roped me in to help because they were short-staffed, and that work not only kept me busy but also got me high visibility with folks I didn't know before. It got me interested in different work areas and helped me later when it was time to pursue a new role. People saw me going beyond my core work area, and that had the dual benefit of showing I was good at other things and that I wanted to do more. All because I put my hand up and went 1UP.

Now, I know sometimes this is tough, especially when we are already sinking in work—being asked to do and deliver more with less time and money. If this pressure is coming from a toxic work environment, it's worth considering whether this challenge is specific to your team or part of the larger organisational culture. If it is the former, then all the more reason to go 1UP and eventually become the boss who changes things for the better. If it is the latter, that is probably not the place to go 1UP. That is the place to plot your exit from as soon as possible.

Go 1 UP! What are you waiting for?

Outworking Versus Working Out

There are times when you want to outwork the other person simply because it gets you ahead in a competitive environment. It can also bring some amazing ideas to the fore, with the objective being for you to win. Think of a race for a promotion where you know it's between you and a few others. You have to outwork them with rock-solid, outstanding work—putting in the extra hours, going the extra mile, and thinking and working consistently and smartly to win the race.

Then, there are times when you want to work out the problem, simply because it makes things better in a complicated world. It also brings some amazing ideas to the fore, with the objective being for everyone to win. Think of this as a promotion where the race is to solve a big problem that can make a significant difference to your team, project, and organisation.

Both approaches are valuable in different contexts and recognising when to apply each is a key part of professional growth. I am encouraging you to be aware of both and ask yourself if you are doing each to the best of your ability.

Know when to outwork and when to work out—both are essential and equally important.

More from Less

'What will it take to get it done?' This is the question we get asked most by the boss when I or my team present a new idea or problem-solving proposal. And the expected answer, as I have learnt the hard way, is not 'give me more money, more people, and more time', but rather how we can smartly do it by:

- Reprioritising existing resources, ensuring that the folks working on those feel more important now, not less.
- Stopping initiatives that are not working by letting go of pet projects or ego-driven endeavours.
- Borrowing from other parts of the business that are doing well by making them part of the success story.

Know that working with a frugal approach to deliver results is what the boss wants. That is what gets you noticed as well. Most teams can deliver more with more, but can you deliver more with less? That is the pragmatic reality of most businesses, and that is what the boss is looking for.

I learnt this when I joined the business in Kenya. The clear brief from my boss was, 'Pawan, your success equals you doubling the business turnover in three years.' And so, our journey began. Everything that worked was counter to what you would normally expect. I had to reduce the number of brands we supported, reduce the number of initiatives we were doing, and reduce pretty much everything. Why? Because more from the core is better than more from more. With fewer brands to support, we focused on fewer, bigger actions. We focused on consistency and continuity, not creation and confusion. Developing one TV asset that worked for consistency and airing it for years, even as we got bored of our work much sooner than consumers did. We cleverly optimised the number of variants and pack sizes we sold, focusing on the bestsellers and the core versus the niche, reducing the time it took to order, plan, manufacture, and sell. We 'fed' the most important brands first, ensuring they were fully supported, and if nothing was left for the tail brands, so be it. We optimised the team size to get the right people to focus on the right work, increasing their span of responsibility and making them feel more empowered, confident, and serious about their roles. And at every step, being in sync with my boss on knowing, 'What will it take to get this done?' and ensuring that happened, come what may. All of this led to the results being achieved in the end, along with many unforgettable lessons for life.

The simple reality of business is that you have to learn how to deliver more with less. Entrepreneurs and families stretching their budgets get this instinctively, but managers typically struggle with it. Treat your organisation's money and time like your own and experience the joy of doing more with less—it is a whole new high.

Can you deliver more with less?

Winning Support: Align to Shine

A big formal session with key stakeholders is probably not the best place to present your big idea as the next big thing. Getting key stakeholders aligned beforehand will get you more buy-in, as you can understand their thoughts and concerns, address them, and get them on your side. It seems obvious, but many of us try to avoid this step. Or worse, we try to align just the 'big boss', but today, top-down diktats do not work. There will be no ownership of the idea, and you are setting yourself up for failure. Thus, do not try to muscle your idea through as a surprise on the big stage. Build your muscle in the old-fashioned way—by working hard for it, getting everyone on your side, one person at a time, one step at a time.

Why did I include this article in this section? Because a key element of getting ahead is showcasing your big ideas and getting buy-in for them. In my experience, more than the idea itself, it's how the people dynamics, the politics, and the egos are managed smartly that makes the difference between success and failure for both the idea and the person involved.

I remember a part-amusing story here. In one of my recent roles, I wanted to attend a leadership course to improve my leadership ability and be ready for bigger roles in the future. So, imagine my extreme confusion when my boss, upon hearing this, sent me instead to a writing course! Yep, you read that right, an executive writing course to help me write better reports and papers. 'What the . . .?' I thought. But you have got to go when your boss says you have to go, so off I went. And boy, did my jaw drop, my eyes pop wide open, and my brain got rewired. I was taught by folks who wrote for the top magazines in the world, and the 'aha' moment came when they shredded the work I submitted and told me they couldn't really understand what I was trying to say or the objective of the paper(s). And that is when the transformative journey began. Through this course, I learnt how to clarify my own thinking—first in terms of what I want to say, then what I want to achieve with what I communicate—and then how to work hard to express it simply, crisply, and clearly, as that is what people need and want. The greatest leaders and the greatest salespeople are those who can get their story across in this way. Learning the critical art of writing was one of the best gifts of my career and helps me every single day in getting buy-in for my big ideas.

Interestingly, I now greatly appreciate my son's school, where they are actively teaching him how to write papers and stories properly, with structures, rules, hooks, etc. Such a valuable lesson. This is what should be taught in corporate inductions, in addition to the other mandatory sessions.

Get buy-in for your idea one person at a time.

Energise to Excel: The Power of Exercise and Holidays

We live in a world where, with a little bit of credibility and potential, we can borrow from our future selves to pay for what we want today. Whether it's taking a loan to buy a house or swiping a credit card for a holiday booking. But the one thing you cannot borrow from the future is more energy to do more today. That must come from whatever reserves you have today. And you have to learn to build up this energy reserve, while also remembering that it cannot be preserved. Build it up, use it, or lose it.

Those who do well know this and work hard to build their energy reserves, using them to achieve their goals. 'Discipline is the bridge between goals and accomplishment,' said Jim Rohn. I would add, 'Energy is the bridge between determination and discipline.' Building your energy levels and creating a disciplined routine to achieve your goals requires a holistic approach. This includes physical exercise, mental well-being, healthy eating habits, a sense of purpose, and having a clear dream to strive for.

All my best bosses were high on energy that lasted and lasted and lasted, like those bunnies they show in battery advertisements! One common thread in their energy: exercising and holidays! I have seen them resolutely hard-code exercise into their calendars, so it's scheduled, and other things get designed around it. I have seen them remember to exercise, especially when travelling, as that is when this tends to get disrupted. I have seen them take on challenges like competing in races or events to keep the momentum going. I have also seen them tenaciously take holidays, not just to recharge but also to signal to their teams that it's the right thing to do. And they took regular holidays with intent, focused on what they learnt, whether it was lazing by the beach, scuba diving, or going on silent retreats! Interestingly, I have seen people take different kinds of holidays to recharge in different ways, from family holidays to solo getaways to trips with their 'besties', something I am yet to adopt.

Reflecting on their habits, I realised how these practices not only fuelled their personal energy but also amplified their professional effectiveness. This constant focus on keeping their energy up is reflected in their work as well. This has been a big learning for me over the years. At the start of my career, I was hesitant to take holidays and deeply regret it now. My advice to my younger self: exercise every day and take holidays. The world will not stop without you, and you will exponentially increase your energy to do more and achieve more.

Energy is the bridge between determination and discipline.

Pick Up the Hat

When things are simple, there's always someone wanting to wear the leadership hat. Even more so when it's apparent the work is going to be a success. On the other hand, when things are complicated, it's a whole different story. Time and again, I have seen the leadership hat in these situations put on the table, waiting to be worn. Anyone can pick it up and take on the complicated challenge, but very few do. And those that do endure agony before ecstasy, frustration before progress, and go down before they are back up. Honestly, it's not for everyone, but look out for those who dare to take the leadership hat in these situations. They are the ones who will go on to do big things. They are the ones I would work for any day. They are the ones who will make a difference in the end.

True leadership is about stepping up in challenging and uncertain situations, not just when success seems guaranteed.

The Power of 'I Have Got This'

'Leave it with me.' 'Consider it done.' 'Forget about it. I have got this.' These phrases are music to any boss's ears! When you reach the stage where you can confidently say this to your boss about a task, it signals that you have truly arrived and settled into your role.

To say these words with confidence requires the following:

1. **Mastery of Your Skills**

    You must have worked hard to develop the knowledge and expertise needed to deliver results.

2. **Strong Collaboration Abilities**

    Achieving tasks often involves others. It means you have cultivated solid relationships, built trust, and established effective ways of working with colleagues.

3. **Trust from Your Boss**

    Being trusted to handle matters independently reflects your boss's confidence in you—an achievement in itself.

All in all, a critical step in advancing your career is earning the reputation of someone who gets things done, particularly in the moments that matter. Building this trust and reliability takes time and consistent effort, but it's a game-changer when aiming for that next promotion.

Master the art of getting things done.

Key Takeaways

- Sometimes things don't work out, but what truly matters is how you think, respond, and move forward.
- Performance + Potential = Promotion.
- Go 1 UP! What are you waiting for?
- Know when to outwork and when to work out—both are essential and equally important.
- Can you deliver more with less?
- Get buy-in for your idea one person at a time.
- Become a storyteller; folks will listen to whatever you have to say!
- Energy is the bridge between determination and discipline.
- True leadership is about stepping up in challenging and uncertain situations, not just when success seems guaranteed.
- Master the art of getting things done.

10
FIRST-TIME BOSS: WHAT TO EXPECT

Earning Your Stripes as a New Boss

Much like a newbie, you need to earn your stripes as a boss. Those who approach the new role with the humility and curiosity of a newbie, in my experience, do well, as opposed to those who think they know it all and that is why they got promoted!

Navigating the early stages of leadership requires strategic actions and thoughtful decisions. Here's a guide to help you make the most of your new role

1. **The First 100 Days**

    Speak to as many people as you can in your first 100 days—your team members, your peers, your superiors, your customers, and experts in your area of work. The first 100 days are a one-time opportunity to learn unabashedly and ask all kinds of questions. Make the best use of this time. No one expects answers from a new boss in the first 100 days, but they do expect curiosity and questions!

2. **The Second 100 Days**

   Impact first, intent later. Decide what your early wins will look like and aim to achieve them in the second 100 days. In my experience, getting some early wins under your belt within the first six months of taking on a new role as team leader is critical. It shows a bias for action and putting learning into practice. Leave it too late, and you will come across as dithering; do something too quickly, and you will come across as rash. Choose your actions and timing wisely.

3. **The Third 100 Days**

   First, know the rules, then break the rules. This is the phase to reframe and refresh the vision for the team, make personnel changes if needed, and get your team, your peers, and your own boss on your side to achieve greatness.

4. **Have Someone on Your Speed Dial**

   The Godfather had his Consiglieri—who do you have? Having someone who can tell you the truth, call you out when you are going off track, and keep you grounded is critical as you cement your role as a team leader. This could be a friend from another team, a person from HR, your boss, your mentor, or a coach—anyone, but have someone you can reach out to for help and guidance.

As you step into your new role as a boss (hopefully with comfy shoes), remember that leadership is a two-way street; just don't be the one causing the traffic jam. Ask questions and lots of them. Your team will appreciate your curiosity, and trust me, it's far better than pretending to know it all. Once you have gathered enough insight to form a solid point of view, turn it into action. But here's the key: bring everyone along for the journey. After all, great leaders don't just steer the ship; they ensure everyone is rowing in sync (and not jumping overboard!).

Approach leadership with humility, curiosity, and a strategic mindset, using your first 300 days to learn, make an impact, and solidify your role.

The 3Es: A Boss's Quick Check Strategy

Becoming the boss comes with its challenges, especially when you are overseeing markets, units, or factories. How do you quickly gauge if things are on track without drowning in lengthy presentations that may not reflect the real picture?

Here's a strategy I devised when I was a sales manager: Look for the 3Es.

1. End (The Goal)

Is there a clear goal everyone is aware of and working towards? As we have covered earlier, all action is aimless without a goalpost. So, for instance, check if your distributors have specific goals. Those with concrete targets will outperform those chasing vague growth figures.

2. **Engagement (The Team Spirit)**

   A team aligned with a clear goal is unstoppable. You feel their energy and enthusiasm the moment you step into their space. If this vibe is missing, that is a red flag. No amount of resources can substitute for genuine team engagement.

3. **Execution (The Action)**

   This is where the rubber meets the road. Often sidelined, execution is critical. A key indicator is whether the leaders know the nitty-gritty of frontline tasks. Can they step in and handle core business operations themselves? If yes, you are likely looking at a well-oiled machine. If not, there's trouble brewing.

The 3Es have become my indispensable quick-check tool. As leaders with ever-expanding portfolios, these practical heuristics are invaluable for staying intimately connected with the ground reality. At the start of my career, in my first sales stint, I was taught how to thoroughly check for the 3Es, and it has stayed with me ever since. I joined as an area sales manager, and the working rule was: Tuesday to Thursday in the field, and Mondays and Fridays in the office. The days in the field were for vigorously 'rolling up our sleeves' and collaborating closely with the on-ground team on the end goal, engagement, and execution—checking for real challenges and proactively solving them. Fridays in the office were for structuring our thoughts, identifying common challenges, and creating a plan. Mondays were for dynamic team discussions with peers and the boss, and for preparing to head out again.

I share this story because the discipline of being out there where the real action is happening, where tangible value is being added, is critical. Every time I have built a disciplined approach to being out there, things work out. Every time I bury my head behind my laptop at a desk, I struggle. We need to actively exit the desk and enter the vibrant real world to achieve the 3Es!

Use the 3Es—End, Engagement, and Execution—as a practical framework to quickly assess progress and ensure your team is on track to achieve goals.

Coach or Captain?

Sports teams typically have a captain and a coach, and their roles are (mostly) different and clear. While in the corporate world, there's a boss. Now, is the boss the coach or the captain?

In my corporate experience, a boss often takes on the role of either a coach or a captain, depending on the situation. A boss acts as a coach when guiding a new team member, managing a seasoned team of smart individuals working together, or helping someone who feels stuck, whether by offering a broader perspective or leveraging experience to help them move forward. On the other hand, a boss becomes a captain in times of crisis, when strong and decisive leadership is essential, when rebuilding a team from scratch, or when leading the team into completely uncharted territory.

If you try to be a captain when you should be a coach, you will end up stifling the team or not being able to get people to work with each other, and folks might just quit on you. If you try to be a coach when you should be a captain, you might lose the confidence of the team, and the team might lose its way as it won't know how to come together. So, make sure to opt for the role of a coach or a captain based on the situation, adapting your approach to either guide and support or lead and take charge, depending on what the team needs at that moment.

Know when to lead as a coach and when to lead as a captain.

Leading Through Empowerment

Empowerment is a powerful tool. It energises people and makes them excited to come to work. However, to empower effectively, consider the following:

1. **Ensure Proper Training or Skillset**

   Empowerment works only when the team is trained or skilled enough to handle the tasks. Delegating tasks without this foundation is unfair at best and negligent at worst.

2. **Provide Initial Support**

   At the start of any empowerment journey, offer guidance to inspire confidence and help solve problems. Challenges are inevitable, and it's essential to reinforce belief early on.

3. **Clarify Your Value**

   As a leader, be clear on what value you are adding to both the team and the tasks at hand. Your role in the empowerment process is to guide and support, not just delegate.

Neglecting any of these steps may result in failing to empower, and instead, abandoning your responsibility as a leader. Let me illustrate these principles with a story from my first stint as a sales manager.

As a young sales manager, I led a team where everyone was older than me (many nearly twice my age). They had extensive experience in their roles and a deep understanding of the sales area. In those early months, I could feel all eyes on me, watching how I would handle challenges. I quickly realised I couldn't match their experience or local knowledge. Instead, I focused on how I could help them in their jobs and careers. One day, I shared my marketing and strategy insights, demonstrating how they could apply these concepts in their day-to-day work. This act of adding value before expecting anything in return marked a noticeable shift in our working relationship.

A unique aspect of this team was that they were unionised, with fixed salaries rather than the typical sales incentive structure. This challenged my assumption that incentives are the primary driver of behaviour. I discovered that their motivation stemmed from a desire to showcase their expertise and skills, which enhanced their self-worth and earned them respect in their community.

Key learnings from this experience:

1. Respect collective wisdom and earn respect by adding value.
2. As a boss, do something for others before expecting anything in return.
3. Understand what drives motivation. It isn't always about monetary rewards; autonomy and recognition can be powerful motivators.

4. Start with trust, not mistrust, especially when working with experienced team members.
5. Acknowledge the whole picture. Recognise not just your team members but also their families, who play a crucial role in supporting a salesperson's success.

The biggest takeaway: Being a boss comes with power and privilege; use it to spread kindness and help people feel better, do better, and achieve more in their lives. This experience taught me invaluable lessons about empowerment, trust, and recognition. It showed me that effective leadership goes beyond delegation to truly empowering team members and appreciating their value.

Empowerment is most effective when combined with training, support, and guidance.

Leading with Fear or Hope?

As a leader, you can achieve results either through fear or respect. Some bosses rely on fear—commanding authority, making decisions without explanation, and demanding compliance without room for dissent. This approach, rooted in control, may seem effective in the short term but risks eroding trust and morale over time. On the other hand, there are leaders who inspire respect by treating their teams with dignity, engaging in open dialogue, and mentoring them for growth. These leaders lead by example, earning trust through their actions and fostering a culture of mutual respect and collaboration.

Similarly, when delivering tough messages, there are two ways to approach the situation: one is focused on the consequences of failure, which instils fear and inaction; the other highlights the vision of success, which empowers the team to move forward with resolve. While fear can motivate temporarily, its effects diminish over time. In contrast, fostering a fearless attitude driven by hope and a clear vision can lead to sustained progress and stronger team dynamics. Ultimately, the most effective leaders know when to motivate with respect and inspiration, ensuring that fear does not become the default tool for driving action.

Inspiring hope and showing a clear vision of success will foster long-term motivation and resilience.

The Power of Vocal Support

If you are the boss supporting a new project, be outspoken and vocal in your support. Why? Here are three key reasons:

1. **New Initiatives Challenge the Status Quo**
   Companies often encourage employees to follow established norms and processes, which means new projects frequently face resistance. When you champion a new initiative, you are not just disrupting the routine; you are giving your team permission to break free from the usual grind. It's like encouraging them to colour outside the lines because who wants to live in a black-and-white world?

2. **The Naysayers Will Emerge**

   In most organisations, multiple stakeholders are involved in approving new initiatives, creating potential roadblocks. New projects, by their nature, venture into uncharted territory, making it easy for critics to highlight risks, predict failures, and stall progress. You can almost hear the chorus of 'What ifs?' echoing through the room! By being vocal in your support, you not only silence the naysayers but also inspire your team to focus on solutions instead of obstacles. After all, every great idea was once met with scepticism, just ask anyone who tried to convince their friends that pineapple belongs on pizza!

3. **The Bigger Picture Is Often Overlooked**

   As you move up the hierarchy, long-term planning takes precedence over short-term execution. Your ability to see the broader vision, informed by experience and strategic focus, is essential for guiding the project. While your team might be absorbed in the finer details, it's your role to remind them why they embarked on this journey in the first place. Think of yourself as the captain of a ship. While the crew navigates through choppy waters, you are keeping an eye on the horizon, steering toward smoother seas ahead.

To conclude, your visible and vocal support as the boss ensures that the team stays aligned with the project's goals and remains committed to delivering results. When you lead with enthusiasm and clarity, you transform potential roadblocks into stepping stones for success.

Visible and vocal support from the boss is crucial in overcoming resistance, aligning the team, and ensuring the success of new initiatives.

Based on My Experience . . .

In most corporate discussions, I have found that prefacing your point with phrases like, 'This is my view/opinion . . .' or 'My assumption/inference is...' can be incredibly effective. As a boss, this approach is crucial because it fosters a safe space for discussion and debate, rather than pressuring the team to follow your direction blindly. Using such phrases encourages open dialogue, prevents putting others on the defensive (and triggering fight-or-flight reactions), and leaves room for you to adjust your perspective.

Moreover, when a new boss steps in, the team's natural instinct is to wonder, 'What does the new boss want, and can I deliver on that?' This often leads to blindly following orders without proper scrutiny. But when a boss invites challenges, explains their reasoning, and frames discussions to include other perspectives, good things happen.

I learnt this the hard way during one of my stints as a new boss. Buoyed by the success of a previous role, I stepped into a stagnant business scenario with a 'know-it-all' attitude. I conducted onboarding presentations, customer visits, and one-on-one meetings with key stakeholders and diligently crafted a plan. But it just didn't click with the team. Why? Two reasons:

1. I came in with an 'I am here to save the business' mentality. This rarely works and was a misstep born of my initial enthusiasm.
2. The team already knew the real reasons behind the business struggles. They needed someone to truly listen, understand, and brainstorm solutions. If the fixes were simple, they would have implemented them already.

Instead, I presented my opinions as facts, my deductions as confirmed hypotheses, and my biases as strengths. Unsurprisingly, it failed. Thankfully, during an off-site, the team confronted me and pointed out why my approach wasn't working. That intervention cleared the fog in my brain, and we essentially had a second start.

What followed was remarkable: the same team, the same leader, but a completely different dynamic. The business doubled in growth over the next few years. External recognition soared, career advancements multiplied, and most importantly, team engagement and the joy of collaboration reached new heights.

To conclude, my single piece of advice is to always start with this: 'This is my view, based on my experience, biases, and blind spots, and I could be wrong . . .' By explicitly stating your potential biases and blind spots, you will help the team understand your thought process and create a safe space for pushback and collaboration.

Preface your views with openness and humility to encourage collaboration, diverse perspectives, and trust.

Don't Leave It Almost Done

In the corporate world, most work is highly interdependent, and even small progress on complex topics takes considerable effort. From informal alignments to strategic approvals, formal sign-offs, and then realising a boss has changed (forcing you to start over) to delays caused by shifting external realities or evolving technology, getting significant things done at work is challenging. That is why I sigh when I see people leaving things nearly finished, assuming they will somehow get completed. They won't. Those tasks will linger just shy of the finish line or, worse, start sliding backwards. It is like those last ten unopened boxes after moving house which are still sitting unopened to this day, aren't they? Thus, it's important to realise that pushing something from 0 to 98 per cent doesn't mean momentum will automatically carry it to 100 per cent. There's no such thing as work momentum; what exists is work inertia.

The people who stand out and make a mark are those who excel at moving work from 98 to 100 per cent. They don't slack off; they lean in, identify and resolve every issue, and don't let fatigue take over. These individuals shift from leading from the back to leading from the front, ensuring the work gets across the finish line. They are the star players who don't get substituted at the 89th minute of a football game after scoring two goals; instead, they stay for the full time and extra time to see the job through. Moreover, as a boss, having the mindset to stay in the game and see things through to the end is absolutely essential. That is how you truly earn your stripes.

An effective boss moves the work from 98 to 100%.

The Power of Breaks: Leading by Example

A big part of being a boss is taking care of your team. This means creating an environment where the team can thrive at work. Timely breaks and vacations are a critical part of this. Furthermore, take a break yourself as a boss, and you will send the right message. Encourage your team to take regular breaks, too. Avoid placing conditions on these breaks—trust their intent and ensure the rest of the team is aligned and capable of handling the workload in their absence.

In the early years of my career, I took breaks very sporadically. Growing up, we had school breaks, but these were mostly spent at home playing or, as I got older, studying. At university, breaks were often consumed by internships. And at work, the desire to start strong led to complete focus on the job, with no real planned vacations. Weekends were usually a blur of drinking, watching movies, or napping, and longer breaks happened only on a whim. It was only later that I started thinking and planning my breaks more systematically, and it has been life-changing. Thoughtful planning has allowed me to save and spend wisely on holidays I truly wanted, visiting places when it made the most sense.

From safaris in Africa to trekking on active volcanoes in Iceland, cruising down the Nile, or visiting a remote island in Australia, these trips happened almost exactly as I envisioned them. And as my family grew from one to two to three and then four, I learnt that smart planning when you are young lets you do what you want, when you want. Leave it too late, and other factors—financial constraints, school schedules (if you have kids), or urgent work challenges—get in the way.

Finally, if you take proper breaks as a boss, your team is likely to follow your lead. If you don't lead by example, no matter what you say, people may feel uneasy about taking time off when they see you constantly working. Fortunately,

I have been blessed with bosses who took their breaks and enthusiastically encouraged their teams to do the same. This created a happy and energised team environment.

Take thoughtful breaks and ensure your team does the same.

How to Lead When the Going Gets Tough

If you think you are an amazing boss on a bright, sunny, winning day, you probably are! But take a moment to reflect on how you behaved when things were challenging. Did you absorb all the stress, suffering silently while your team remained unaware, only to pay the price of being a sponge? Or did you offload all the stress onto your team, watch them struggle, and eventually pay the price of being a wide-open gate?

The truth is that tough times reveal your true character. In my experience, when faced with challenging situations:

1. **Be Honest with the Team**

    Sugarcoating reality doesn't help. The goal is to get everyone on board to find a way forward—or to identify those who need to step off.

2. **Be Honest with Your Boss**

    Clearly outline your views, options, challenges, and the chances of success or failure. Consistency and honesty win over suspense and sporadic successes.

3. **Help and Ask for Help**

   Dive into the work, valuing ideas over hierarchy. Avoid phrases like, 'I don't care how, but get it done' or 'Make it happen, no matter what.' Such statements often lead good people to make bad choices under pressure.

4. **Trust and Respect Your Team**

   Be okay with whatever happens, and take ownership of the outcomes, especially failures. That is your role as the decision-maker. The perks and risks come as a package—embrace both.

5. **Seek Feedback**

   Ask your team and peers for their insights. This can teach you a lot about your behaviour and its impact.

6. **Invest in Self-awareness Tools**

   Tools like the strength deployment inventory (SDI) help analyse your motivations, values, and how your behaviour changes in conflict situations. Doing this when times are good and discussing it as a team can prepare everyone better for challenging days.

Personally, I have found these approaches to be incredibly effective in creating a solid foundation that supports both the team and the leader during challenging times.

During challenging times, choose honesty, collaboration, and self-awareness to strengthen both your team and yourself.

Key Takeaways

- Approach leadership with humility, curiosity, and a strategic mindset, using your first 300 days to learn, make an impact, and solidify your role.
- Use the 3Es—End, Engagement, and Execution—as a practical framework to quickly assess progress and ensure your team is on track to achieve goals.
- Know when to lead as a coach and when to lead as a captain.
- Empowerment is most effective when combined with training, support, and guidance.
- Inspiring hope and showing a clear vision of success will foster long-term motivation and resilience.
- Visible and vocal support from the boss is crucial in overcoming resistance, aligning the team, and ensuring the success of new initiatives.
- Preface your views with openness and humility to encourage collaboration, diverse perspectives, and trust.
- An effective boss moves the work from 98 to 100%.
- Take thoughtful breaks and ensure your team does the same.
- During challenging times, choose honesty, collaboration, and self-awareness to strengthen both your team and yourself.

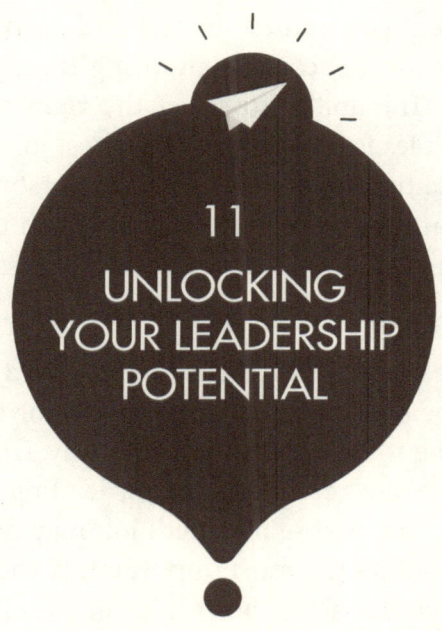

11
UNLOCKING YOUR LEADERSHIP POTENTIAL

First Who, Then What: Leadership Fundamentals

Have you ever wondered what truly separates great leaders from the rest when it comes to leading and managing their teams? Through experience, I have identified three key lessons that could transform the way you think about leadership. These insights might just be the game-changer you need to elevate your approach and inspire those around you. Here's a brief outline of these principles that can define your success as a leader.

1. **First Who, Then What**

    I borrowed the term 'first who, then what' from the book *Good to Great* by Jim Collins, which explains what makes great companies survive and thrive. One of the first mantras of success is choosing the right people for the team. The ability to select the right individuals for different roles is probably the toughest job a leader faces. Taking the time to choose the right person for the job—even if it means enduring the short-term pain of leaving roles vacant—is a critical marker of success.

2. **Cut the Rope**

    Sometimes, you need to cut the rope and let people go. It could be because they are not right for the role or not performing to expectations. Either way, failing to act will demotivate the rest of the team, leading to a lose-lose situation. This part of a leader's job may not be the most pleasant, but it's the most important. If you don't want to make tough decisions, don't take on a leadership role. As Uncle Ben wisely told Peter Parker in *Spider-Man*, 'With great power comes great responsibility.'

3. **Embrace Your First Follower**

    There's a wonderful TED talk by Derek Silvers called 'How to Start a Movement', where he highlights the importance of the first follower. He says, 'The first follower is what transforms a lone nut into a leader.' He is absolutely right. As a leader, when you outline your vision, strategy, and plan, you need supporters, and that starts with the first follower. The first follower legitimises your approach. A second follower joins in, then more, and soon you have the team on board—all because of the first follower. Embrace your first follower and respect what they bring to your plan.

I remember when I went to Ethiopia and had to start hiring people to join the team. The first challenge was that our organisation wasn't well-known in the country as we had no operations there. Then there was the issue of not having an office (at that time), nothing being manufactured yet, and no clear guarantees of the future, which made it hard to show potential candidates a career path. This situation made it clear that those who would want to join had to be risk-takers, willing to take second chances, comfortable with uncertainty, proactive, able to navigate ups and downs, and driven by a sense of purpose and determination. And then it began—searching through LinkedIn, contacts, advertising, and recruitment agencies. We ended up with a huge list to start with. I spent hours and hours interviewing (at one point, more than fifty candidates for one role), shortlisting, and interviewing again as the list narrowed. And boy, was it worth it.

It took some time, even after we selected the right people, simply because we didn't have an office address to issue offer letters or tell people where to report (that is a separate story!). Today, many of the senior leaders in the country are the very same people we hired at the start of the journey—one reason being the maniacal focus on 'first who, then what'. I read this concept early in my career, and the mantra has stayed with me ever since. Time and again, I have seen it play out. It is tough to leave a position vacant and manage the challenges that come with it, but it's worth the search for the right people. The long-term benefits of having the right people in the right roles far outweigh the short-term pain of managing vacancies. A valuable tip is to consistently engage and nurture your network, building a list of potential candidates as you never know when that will come in handy. It goes without saying that your own reputation as a boss and a team member will ultimately make the difference in whether these awesome people will choose to work for you. Look into the mirror every day and ask yourself: Does anyone have you on their list of people to hire, and are you on the list of bosses people want to work for?

The right people, decisive actions, and a loyal first follower are the foundation of leadership success.

Influencing Versus Imposing

At the initial stages of our careers, we have no choice but to influence if we want others to buy into our ideas. This is also when we experience the most satisfaction, when our ideas or suggestions are accepted. But as we progress in our careers, the temptation to impose our will can become alluring. As the boss or senior leader, we may feel entitled to simply dictate tasks and expect compliance. But is it truly that simple? While direct reports may comply, what about those who don't report to us but are crucial to success? Moreover, even with our direct reports, adopting an authoritarian stance can be perilous. It stifles feedback, hinders the refinement of ideas, and deprives us of valuable discussions that could enhance our plans.

Ultimately, it all boils down to influence as the only viable option. There's no sustainable alternative. Remember that progress depends on the merit of ideas, not the seniority of the individuals behind them. It is about rallying support based on the strength and value of the idea itself, rather than relying on positional authority. Let me conclude this section with a story that vividly illustrates the power of influence over imposition.

In March 2020, as COVID-19 rapidly spread across the globe, we faced a critical challenge in Kenya: the urgent need for sanitisers. With imports no longer feasible, we had to find a local solution and fast. This crisis demonstrated why influencing is more effective than imposing, even under high-pressure circumstances. As a leader, I learnt to embrace vulnerability, trust in collective wisdom, and make the challenge personal for everyone involved. Instead of dictating a course of action, I facilitated a lengthy video call and brainstorming session, encouraging open dialogue and considering every suggestion. The result was remarkable. In just fifteen days, we moved from concept to execution—finding a local manufacturer, sourcing materials, and navigating safety and regulatory approvals. This rapid success wasn't achieved through top-down directives but through influence and collaboration.

It is important to note that my role wasn't that of an authoritarian figure issuing orders but of a storyteller inspiring action and supporting the team every step of the way. This approach embodied the principle of influence over imposition, proving that progress hinges on the merit of ideas, not the seniority of individuals.

The power of influence became evident in how the first supporter of an idea sparked a cascade effect, encouraging others to contribute and speak up. This positive momentum grew organically, without the need for hierarchical pressure. Even in a crisis, rallying support through the strength and value of ideas proved far more effective than relying on positional authority.

Ultimately, this experience reinforced the most important leadership lesson: true leadership isn't about a boss leading a team; it's about creating an environment where the team can lead itself. By trusting the team to step up, offering opportunities for members to exceed expectations (go 1UP), and fostering an atmosphere where leadership can emerge from anywhere, we achieved what once seemed impossible.

This story serves as a testament to an earlier point: influencing isn't just preferable; it's the only sustainable path to effective leadership, no matter the situation or urgency.

The key is to influence, not impose.

Stay With Me

A leader, by definition, is someone who has followers. Followers, by definition, follow the leader. If you are a leader, always ask yourself if you are doing what is needed for people to follow you. Just being a boss or manager does not make you a leader. Are you caring for your team? Are you taking care of your team? Are you protecting them when needed? Are you taking the blame and giving them the credit? Are you leading them in the right direction? Are you sharing hope and hiding your fears? Are you inspiring them to work, rather than scaring them into working? Are you ready for all the sacrifices a leader must make?

And if you are a follower, ask yourself if you truly believe in your leader. Are you doing what it takes to take care of your leader? Are you living up to the expectations? Are you patient enough to tide over the rough patches? Are you ready to go where the leader takes you?

In my career, I have collaborated with people I would gladly work with again on any project. One shared quality among all of them was their ability to speak the truth to me—directly, plainly, and consistently. Let me share a few episodes that highlight the same.

There was this one time, during my very first sales stint, when I thought I was stuck on a particular part of the project, only to be bluntly told by my boss that it was my mindset that was stuck, not the project. Boom! Another time, I applied for a role at a company where the boss made it clear: working for him meant no work-life balance, long, gruelling hours, demanding targets, and constantly shifting, high-pressure challenges. The payoff? A high-risk, high-reward career opportunity. And guess what? I took it. But I knew what I was walking into and aced it, thanks to the frank and honest job requirements being outlined. On another occasion, my boss candidly told me that while my analytical skills were strong, my ability to work with a multicultural, multinational team needed improvement if I wanted to achieve my goals. He offered to personally invest in helping me grow in this area, and that made all the difference in my work and outcomes.

In all these situations, my bosses showed that they cared about me personally, supported me, and gave me honest feedback from the beginning. Because of this, I would happily work with them again on any project.

As a leader, do you possess the qualities that will inspire people to follow you anywhere?

Great Leaders Are Great Storytellers

Stories help us make sense of what is happening around us, whether in understanding life in general or in our workplace. And if there's no narrative, no story to begin with, it leads to chaos and paralysis in action as people try to make sense of what is happening around them. This can lead to aimlessness and randomness in actions and impact, and I have seen this happen time and time again.

But here's the thing: stories aren't just about making sense of the world; they are about driving change. Logic makes us think; emotions make us act. That's why learning to tell stories is so powerful. Narratives and numbers together form an art that great leaders master and deploy to great effect. So, how can you become a great storyteller? Start by identifying the core message you want to convey—what's the 'why' behind your story? Next, weave in personal anecdotes or relatable experiences that resonate with your audience to create an emotional connection. Finally, practice delivering your story with enthusiasm and authenticity. This way, your passion will be contagious!

Remember, the right story doesn't just explain where you are going; it inspires your team to join you on the journey. So, craft your narrative, share it with confidence, and watch as you transform your leadership style!

A well-crafted narrative helps leaders calm nerves, provide clarity, and drive purposeful action.

(This post was inspired by an insightful point shared by Sir John Hegarty on LinkedIn.)

Evolving as a Leader: Moving Beyond Past Experiences

We have all encountered that boss who constantly rehashes old ideas and repeats the same stories from past experiences in meetings. The truth is, when you are in a leadership role, it's easy to think you have seen it all and know everything, but this mindset limits your growth. Relying on past experiences makes you stagnant and eventually redundant. To stay relevant, it's important to remain open to new ideas—watch new movies and documentaries, engage with different people, disconnect from your phone, etc.

So, the next time you find yourself saying, 'When I was in . . .,' 'When I was your age . . .,' 'Back in the good old days . . .,' or 'I once did this . . .,' pause for a moment and ask yourself whether what you are saying is truly relevant, or if you are just leaning on your past because you haven't made time to learn anything new.

Stay curious and avoid rehashing the past out of habit.

None of the Above

A boss taught me long ago to choose 'none of the above' if none of the options presented suited the needs. There might be more options, hybrid options, or even the option of not doing anything or doing all the above. This approach helps avoid typical traps, such as when agencies or teams present a bad option to make their preferred option look good, or when a high-priced option is introduced to make the middle option seem like better value for money. So, always remember that it's okay to choose 'none of the above' and challenge and inspire better thinking. And if you can explain why clearly and outline your expectations equally clearly, it will help the next iteration improve.

PS: Be clear on whether the situation requires a gold standard solution that may take multiple iterations and time, or a pragmatic solution that is not the best but good enough for now. That feedback helps.

It is okay not to be okay with any of the options.

Everything at Work Is Personal

The common thread in my best work over the years has been powerful emotions—sometimes positive, sometimes not so positive. As a boss, a project leader, and a contributing team member, I have found that sharing the emotions you are feeling and stirring up the right emotions leads to far more amazing outcomes than just sharing logic, contractual obligations, or evidence based on facts. The joy of appreciation, the shame of punishment, the pride of achieving something big, the disappointment of losing to competition . . . it is all personal and emotional. So next time something is stuck at work, explore emotions, not just data.

In my stint in Africa, my boss started something called 'Epic Fail'. This was to address the shame or guilt one feels when a project fails. In a competitive world, it's difficult to accept failure. Expectations are high, the business needs the idea to work, and your career is at stake—all these factors lead to very human behaviours like hiding what is not working, blaming external circumstances, delaying warning signals, and not questioning assumptions. My boss's idea of Epic Fail was to create a safe space in our big monthly gatherings and encourage people to open up about where they had failed. She started by sharing her own failures in the first session, which led a few brave folks to open up, and then it was a catharsis! People realised that others had failed, and that they were not alone. They saw the real faces behind the façade of confidence we often project at work. Folks learnt from each other, figured out what not to do in the future, and gained the confidence to question assumptions and highlight risks earlier.

Here's an example of my own Epic Fail. I pushed my team to launch a petroleum jelly sachet to drive affordability, based on what I thought was a smart analysis of a need-gap in the market. And it flopped. The sachet didn't have a re-sealing mechanism, so once opened, the leftover jelly would leak. An obvious flaw and failure, you might say. But in the narrowed vision of work, believing in your own story, and being the boss, you ignore the tell-tale signs, and that is what happened to me.

When I shared this story in that forum, it was a catharsis for me. There was no intellectual reasoning on why it failed, just an honest admission of stupidity. And instead of being shamed, my boss was okay, folks were supportive, and they shared their stories. We all learnt, and I didn't feel alone, and I didn't have to wallow in misery by myself. That ability to just say it out loud and let it go in public had a profound impact on my future work (with more successes and fewer failures, thankfully).

Emotions are a powerful force in the workplace, capable of influencing both success and failure.

The Company Does Not Care About You

An important lesson I have learnt is that the company itself doesn't care about you; it's the people within it who do. A company itself does not have emotions; it is the people in the company who have emotions. A company does not have values; it is the people in the company who hold values. Thus, a strong company culture emerges when everyone in the organisation shares common beliefs and acts in alignment with those values. This collective mindset shapes how individuals behave and interact, ultimately defining the work environment.

I have observed three key practices that can make this alignment work effectively:

1. Hire people who believe in and have values aligned with what the organisation has or desires. It is much easier to make things happen when this alignment is in place, compared to hiring only for skills and experience and hoping that the values can be superimposed. Values are in the DNA—they cannot be changed. Skills are like clothes—they can be changed.
2. Do not tolerate behaviour that does not align with the values, particularly at the top levels. This is similar to the broken windows theory, which states that visible signs of crime create an environment that encourages further crime. The same applies to values and behaviours. If deviations are tolerated, it signals to the rest of the organisation that it's okay to deviate, which can have a massive negative impact. Nipping deviations in the bud has the opposite and positive effect.

3. Appreciate those who truly live their behaviours and go above and beyond in their line of duty. There are always people like this in organisations—they are the true heroes. Appreciating them not only motivates them but also sends strong signals to the organisation about what the true north star of living the values through behaviour really means. This encourages others to do more, based on trust and confidence that what they are doing is right.

Be the boss who cares and creates a culture of care within your team.

Best Boss = Best Value + Best Values

My most effective achievements at work have come when I have worked with amazing bosses. The best of them brought two things to the table: they were superb at their job based on their experience and expertise, and they were superb at their job in the values they lived—being honest, fair, trustworthy, and creating psychological safety. And they were like that from the word go. That is what consistently set them apart from the others.

And though it's true that we do not get to choose our bosses, if you get a boss with the best values, make the most of that time. If you get the opposite, bail out as soon as practically possible, as it will be the worst time otherwise. And if, by some strange twist of fate, you get to choose, my experience has taught me to choose the better boss over a seemingly better job. But that is just me, maybe.

So, to become a great boss, focus on excelling in your work and living up to strong values. Be the kind of leader you always wished you had.

Values + Value = Visionary leadership..

> **Key Takeaways**
>
> ➤ The right people, decisive actions, and a loyal first follower are the foundation of leadership success.
> ➤ The key is to influence, not impose.
> ➤ As a leader, do you possess the qualities that will inspire people to follow you anywhere?
> ➤ A well-crafted narrative helps leaders calm nerves, provide clarity, and drive purposeful action.
> ➤ Stay curious and avoid rehashing the past out of habit.
> ➤ It is okay not to be okay with any of the options.
> ➤ Emotions are a powerful force in the workplace, capable of influencing both success and failure.
> ➤ Be the boss who cares and creates a culture of care within your team.
> ➤ Values + Value = Visionary leadership.

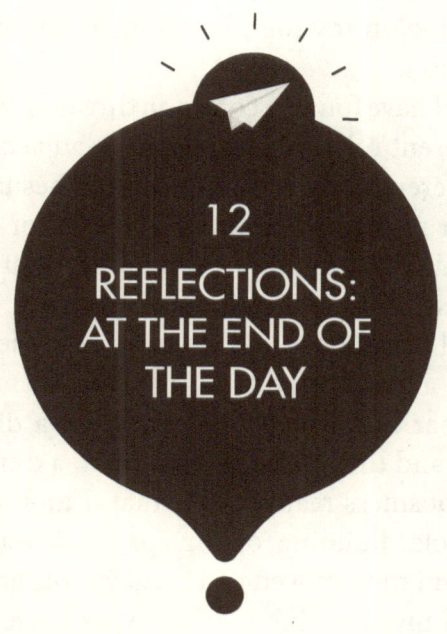

12
REFLECTIONS: AT THE END OF THE DAY

Specialist or Generalist?

If you love the organisation you work in and want to be there for a long time, be a generalist. Broaden your experience by taking on as many different roles as possible early in your career. Be ready to do some roles you love and others that the organisation will ask you to do. On the other hand, if you love the exact function you are in, and it's the one thing that excites you, be a specialist. This means deepening your expertise in that function as early as possible in your career and being ready to move across organisations to pursue what you love. As for me, I am a generalist by choice. I love new adventures, new experiences, and I don't like doing the same thing again. I tend to get complacent and thus, pursuing new things keeps me on my toes, keeps my excitement high, and fuels my passion.

Over time, I have found a common thread in what I am good at across different roles. I have moved to adjacent roles rather than very different ones, as people tend to hesitate to hire you (especially for mid/senior roles) if you aim for something far removed from what you have been doing. That is the trick to being a successful generalist, in my experience. I moved from an entry-level frontline sales role to an entry-level marketing role, then to a trade marketing role (adjacent to sales and marketing), back to a bigger sales role in a different region and division, and then on to marketing in a different country, culture, and business reality. After that, I took a mini general managerial role, building on my past sales and marketing experience, and then moved to a strategy role at headquarters, leveraging all my frontline market experience. The common factor? Moving from one square to an adjacent one.

As for my wonderful friends who built their careers as specialists, they made the choice early on in their professional lives—some right after college, and others after experimenting with different roles, eventually finding what they loved and sticking to it through thick and thin, working to be the best in their chosen area. Beyond this, there are extraneous factors that come into play. You might want or need to stay in a particular place for personal reasons, and that will impact your choices. Your partner's career may necessitate a different discussion about your options. Your kids' age and educational requirements may nudge you to decide based on their needs . . . the list goes on. That's life. The real lesson here is recognising that these factors also play a role in your choices. It's like making decisions in a chess game of life—each move must account for various pieces to achieve success.

> Career success depends on aligning your choices—whether as a generalist or a specialist—with your personal passions, circumstances, and life's broader realities.

Rekindling the Intern Mindset

The corporate journey starts with the new trainee who flirts with questions, is an idealist, and a contrarian thinker. Over time, they evolve into a cynical junior manager and eventually become a pragmatic middle manager in a few years. This is where the tipping point comes in. As one climbs the proverbial corporate ladder, the ability to influence change increases. Those who aspire to become great CEOs need to shift their mindset—from pragmatism back to asking questions, becoming idealists, and embracing contrarian thinking once again!

Every time I see great CEOs, I see their trainee avatar still within them. If you are an intern today or just starting your career, don't lose the habit of asking questions and being an idealist. It will serve you well over time. It's the secret skill you already possess to rise to the top.

So, approach each day with the mindset of an intern—eager to learn, open to new experiences, and ready to embrace challenges. Never stop being curious, asking questions, and striving to grow, no matter where you are in your journey.

> Retain the curiosity, idealism, and questioning mindset of a trainee, no matter how far you climb the ladder.

Forgot What You Did Today?

Ever had that feeling at the end of the day where you struggle to remember exactly what you did at work? Or, if asked what significant thing you achieved or got done today or yesterday, you have to scratch your head to recall. If this happens far too often, maybe it's time to change how you approach your day and set yourself at least one significant task to accomplish. Not just any task—something that will help move your work forward and leave you feeling proud at the end of the day.

Try doing this and write down every day the one thing you accomplished that you are happy about. The more you do this, the more you will be inspired to start your day by focusing on that one big thing to add to your list by the end of the day. Over time, this simple practice will transform your mindset, fuelling your days with purpose and a sense of accomplishment.

Do one big thing today.

Cutting Ribbons or Leaving a Legacy?

From time immemorial, most of the working population has done the same thing day after day, month after month, year after year. Whether in the agricultural era, the industrial era, or even now, it's the same. Then there were the few lucky ones who had the ability, willingness, and good fortune to do whatever they wanted. They spent their time honing their craft and building masterpieces—whether monuments, art pieces, books, or systems. They left behind a legacy. They are the people we talk about even today.

Cut to today, folks like you and me are the lucky ones now. Yet, in our jobs, there's a strong urge to keep shifting from role to role, sometimes even company to company, in a quixotic quest for fame, glory, and money. What gets lost in all of this is the quest to leave a legacy. Thus, it's important to realise that true greatness is staying the course, not cutting the ribbon, and moving on! That's when you will build your masterpiece. That's when you will likely find greater meaning in your job. That's when you will leave a legacy. One of the main reasons I worked for twenty-one years with one organisation (at the time of writing this book) was its deep-rooted belief in making a real difference in the world we live in. It came to the fore during my eight years in East Africa. Two of my favourite brands to work on were Lifebuoy, our soap brand, and Pepsodent, our toothpaste brand. We deployed extensive school outreach programs to educate children on the need to wash their hands and brush their teeth regularly. Every interaction I had with kids in this program made me feel more committed to doing my job better and making an impact. Every year, to build momentum, we organised two massive one-day events on Global Handwashing Day and World Oral Health Day—two specific days recognised by the World Health Organization to remind ourselves of the importance of handwashing and brushing. Looking back at the photos of those events, I see myself at my happiest and most content. The impact we were having was visible in the clean hands and happy smiles of the children. Many people came to the company motivated by the kind of work we did and still do. Being part of those two brands in Ethiopia was one of the most fulfilling and rewarding experiences in my corporate life so far, simply because of the chance to make a difference and leave a mark.

Not everyone is so lucky, but I have met some incredible people who build off their own passion and purpose, bringing that to work to create a movement. If your organisation has a purpose, get involved—that's my advice. If it doesn't, find like-minded people and get started on something that will leave a legacy.

True greatness lies in staying committed to a purpose, leveraging your work to make a meaningful impact, and building a legacy that outlives you.

The Art of Unwinding: Creating Your Decompression Routine

Stress often builds up unconsciously. After a hectic day, it's essential to decompress, much like divers do when resurfacing from deep-sea diving. Establishing a routine to unwind can be incredibly helpful. Consider creating a ritual to signal the end of your workday, such as shutting down your computer, taking a bath before interacting with family, or going for a brief solitary walk. A few minutes of meditation or deep breathing can also help you relax and reset. That small decompression time between stopping work and transitioning to other activities can make a big difference.

My own routines have evolved over time. There was a time when it often involved a glass of wine with dinner and frantic doom-scrolling on my phone. Through trial and error, I stumbled upon a formula that works for me—soothing music, no reading or watching news that aggravates me, charging my phone outside my bedroom, and reading myself to sleep. With constant stimulus and energy coursing through my day, I consciously prioritise seeking tranquillity at night rather than excitement, much like a weary sailor seeking the calm of a harbour.

Find what works for you and follow it. It truly makes a difference.

Establishing a mindful decompression routine helps reset your mind and body.

Be Dissatisfied, Say Thank You, and Repeat

Every morning, wake up with a sense of dissatisfaction—not in a negative way, but in a way that fuels your drive to improve, challenge the status quo, and fight for something better. Let that dissatisfaction push you to act, grow, and work toward the changes you want in your life. But every night, as you lay your head down, shift gears. Say thank you. Be grateful for what you have, the good things in your life, and the effort you put in during the day. Gratitude doesn't mean settling; it means appreciating the present while still striving for more. Then, when morning comes again, let that spark of dissatisfaction return. Use it to propel yourself forward.

Remember, it's about finding the balance by being happy with what you have while never being fully satisfied. That's how progress happens—one grateful night and one determined morning at a time.

Be dissatisfied, say thank you, and repeat.

Bouncing Back from Setbacks

I have had my share of bad days, missed targets, and failed projects. It's easy to wallow in misery, but it's harder to get up and keep going. Over time, I have learnt some hard truths that help:

1. **Distract Yourself**

   Dive into a book, movie, or your favourite hobby. Ignoring those gloomy thoughts is a surefire way to send them packing.

2. **Exercise**

   Physical activity releases feel-good hormones that leave you feeling rejuvenated. Plus, these gloomy guests hate action, so staying active is your best defence against them.

3. **Skip the Booze**

   Contrary to popular belief, alcohol is misery's superfood, not yours. It only makes misery clingier.

4. **Choose Your Confidants Wisely**

   Different friends get different parts of your life. Pick the right one for the right problem.

5. **Embracing the Challenges**

   Another helpful tip when those difficult days come barging in is to remember that it's all part of the journey. As one of my bosses once told me, 'You have got to be in it to win it.'

There was this one job that was my dream job. I thought it had my name all over it. The job description seemed written with me in mind, a bit like how a scriptwriter sometimes writes a movie script with a certain hero in mind. It ticked all the boxes: my experience, my expertise, and how my performance and potential should have led to folks calling me up to offer the job. I am not kidding! I completely and utterly believed this. But as I waited, an announcement email came out, stating that someone else had been appointed to the job (a very good person, to be fair). Furthermore, I wasn't even in the consideration set, let alone perfect for the role. It was one of my worst days at work. Turns out the reasons for not being considered were fair—they wanted someone already doing a similar job at a similar level.

Anyway, I lost it for a while. Disappointment, anger, frustration, crying, and ranting, all came and went. But then something changed. Somewhere in this downward spiral, I vented to my boss, and that helped. For starters, he was a good man who listened to me, and then gave me some tough life lessons on luck, timing, and the importance of staying in the game. He boosted my confidence. Then my personal trainer helped. I used to exercise every morning with a trainer at that time, and he was in no mood to listen to my sob stories—he couldn't care less. All he wanted were push-ups, planks, and bicep curls, and that helped a lot. Getting the anger out on a dumbbell was exactly what I needed! Lastly, it turns out that for my family and friends, all this really didn't matter anyway.

All these strategies helped me snap out of this self-induced misery and get back into the game, with life lessons on not drinking your own Kool-Aid and some wiser lessons on what it takes to get back into the game. Sometimes, failures are crucial stepping stones. They forge resilience and fortitude, ultimately making you stronger.

Distractions + Exercise + Time with Friends = The perfect recipe for banishing the blues.

What Makes for a Good Day at Work?

We all strive for good days at work, but have you ever wondered what truly makes a day great? No, it's not 'Don't go to work!' Instead, it relates to finding your 'why'. Following your passion is an equally good way to avoid having a bad day at work. Your passion is what makes you happy. Finding time every day for this assures you a daily dose of happiness. This idea has been emphasized by numerous thought leaders and resources. Simon Sinek espouses it superbly in his book *Start with Why*, and Prof. Clay Christensen does it beautifully in his article 'How Will You Measure Your Life?'

My purpose is to be a leader and teacher, to leave a long-lasting impact on people, businesses, and the planet. It's the reason I spend time sharing my experiences, working, and doing what I do in my day job. It's also why I am happy but never fully satisfied every day—a great place to be in life, to do more, and live more. And ever since I sharpened my own purpose, it has become my north star, the lifeline that pulls me out of difficult places, leading to every day being a good day. There's never a bad day with purpose! No matter what. Here's a story of how this worked out for me.

I have always wanted to teach within the company, and a while back, in addition to my day job, I took on the role of marketing foundation tutor—an opportunity to formally teach young marketers at the company the basics of marketing. This was a great opportunity to shape young minds. It required dedicated time and effort, and it all just happened. The extra hours didn't add stress, but joy. The additional job didn't increase my burden but increased my satisfaction. At the end of the day, I felt much more useful to the folks around me, which is the greatest gift of all.

As I journey on, a Swahili saying sums it up well: *Haba na haba, hujaza kibaba,* which loosely translates to 'little by little, the pot gets filled'.

Discover and focus on your purpose each day, and you will never have a bad day at work.

Be a Human Being, Not a Human Bin

Stop filling yourself up with unnecessary distractions—be it endless meetings, constant scrolling, too many open tabs, or a flood of opinions from everyone around you. In short, stop being a human bin for all the noise. Instead, open up your time, and be curious, creative, kind, punctual, real, and vulnerable. Be a human being, not a human bin.

So, as you go into your day, try this:

- Share something positive in your meeting.
- Compliment someone you meet today.
- Express gratitude to someone who helped you.
- Help someone unexpectedly.
- Try something new today.

Clear the clutter and focus on being present, kind, and intentional in your interactions to foster meaningful connections and growth.

At the End of the Day

A reflection on twenty-one years of work: how to enjoy what you do and stay happy doing it.

Smile.
Ask how you can help.
Help.

Stand.
Drink.
Breathe.

Show up.
Keep at it.
Repeat.

Do what you say.
Say what you do.
First do, then say.

Be firm.
Be honest.
Be kind.

Time is finite. Wants are infinite. So, think clearly, choose wisely, and act decisively.

Key Takeaways

- Career success depends on aligning your choices—whether as a generalist or a specialist—with your personal passions, circumstances, and life's broader realities.
- Retain the curiosity, idealism, and questioning mindset of a trainee, no matter how far you climb the ladder.
- Do one big thing today.
- True greatness lies in staying committed to a purpose, leveraging your work to make a meaningful impact, and building a legacy that outlives you.
- Establishing a mindful decompression routine helps reset your mind and body.
- Be Dissatisfied, say thank you, and repeat.
- Discover and focus on your purpose each day, and you will never have a bad day at work.
- Clear the clutter and focus on being present, kind, and intentional in your interactions to foster meaningful connections and growth.
- Time is finite. Wants are infinite. So, think clearly, choose wisely, and act decisively.

FRAMEWORKS

'You never really understand a person until you consider things from his point of view.'
—**Atticus Finch**, *To Kill a Mockingbird*

In this section, I share a few frameworks and checklists that have been useful in my life. I don't have too many from a purely practical perspective—less is more, as they say! Use these with caution, as what works for me may not work for you. Feel free to tweak them, adapt them to your needs, or disregard them entirely if they don't align with your thinking. However, I strongly recommend regularly evaluating your past, understanding your present, and preparing for the future. Reflect on your past as a rich learning ground to assess how your choices, circumstances, actions, and attitudes have shaped outcomes. Use your present as a starting point to explore various potential futures and decide which path works best for you. The future, with its myriad possibilities, many of them hopefully positive, is yours to evaluate and shape. Take charge, decide, and zoom ahead!

Measuring Your Life

Purpose = __ / 25
Passion = __ / 25
Work = __ / 25
Family = __ / 25
Total = __ / 100

Take a moment to reflect and rate yourself in these four key areas. This self-assessment is not about perfection but about gaining clarity on where you stand in your life. The idea is to assess how you are doing relative to the overall score of 100. At different times, your scores in these areas will inevitably vary—sometimes high, sometimes low. The key is to focus on improving areas where your score is low while appreciating the areas where it's high. This balance will keep you motivated. The specific sub-parameters you use to calculate your scores are entirely up to you.

I personally perform this check mentally almost every day and take a more detailed look at the end of each year during a relaxed holiday. This practice has helped me set clearer priorities for the year ahead and make timely course corrections in areas where I feel my score is lacking.

Measuring Your Health

Physical health   = __ / 25
Mental health   = __ / 25
Emotional health = __ / 25
Purposeful health = __ / 25
Total   = __ / 100

Achieving a well-rounded and fulfilling life requires intentional effort across different areas. The parameters mentioned above represent key aspects of overall well-being that you should focus on to maintain a healthy and harmonious balance in your life. There's plenty of advice and resources available on this topic, but here's what I have found most effective from my own experience:

- Regular exercise has been the cornerstone of improving every other aspect of my health.
- A healthy, balanced diet and proper sleep have had the most significant impact on my overall well-being.
- Building real social connections while reducing online interactions has also been transformative. I have learnt that a few meaningful relationships are far more fulfilling than a multitude of superficial ones. One important lesson I have realised is the distinction between fun and friendship. You can have fun with people who share a common passion, but that doesn't necessarily make them your friends. True friends genuinely care for you, even if they don't always share the same interests.

- Finally, discovering your passions and purpose—and intentionally dedicating time to them—ensures that no day is truly a bad day. Pursuing something you love adds meaning to your life, and that sense of fulfilment is something no one can take away from you.

Financial Health Framework

A practical reality for most of us is the need to secure both our current and future financial health. A decent life often depends on building strong financial foundations. While each of us has unique circumstances to navigate, here are some common lessons I have learnt over time:

1. Secure your well-being. Invest in health and life insurance for yourself and your loved ones.
2. Save for a rainy day. Aim to have 3-6 months of living expenses saved to handle unexpected layoffs or planned sabbaticals.
3. Spend less than you earn. This is the key to building wealth. If you want to spend more, earn more.
4. Compound your way to wealth. Start saving early in life to harness the power of compounding over time.
5. Borrow but don't burden yourself. Reserve borrowing for meaningful investments in life, not for impulsive purchases like your next pair of jeans.

Tracking Your Personal Brand

Here's a checklist that will help you evaluate your personal brand. In the last one year, have you:

- Have you upskilled seriously? That is, gone beyond reading articles or commenting online by taking courses and tackling new projects in your area of expertise.
- Shared your work and knowledge? That is, tried to communicate your achievements, insights, and learnings to the right people inside and outside your organisation.
- Sought holistic feedback? That is, conducted a 360-degree feedback exercise to gather insights from peers, supervisors, direct reports, and partners to get a well-rounded view of yourself.
- Asked for guidance? That is, regularly sought advice and feedback from your boss beyond the annual appraisal cycle, and actively worked on it.
- Expressed and acted on your intent? That is, clearly articulated your aspirations and taken deliberate steps to work toward them.

If you haven't checked off most of these boxes, don't panic—building your personal brand isn't a sprint; it's more like assembling IKEA furniture: one step at a time, with a few missteps along the way. Pick one area to focus on and take a small but meaningful action. Remember, your brand is shaped by what you do consistently, not by grand gestures.

So, what's your first move? (And no, binge-reading LinkedIn posts doesn't count!)

Buyer Beware

When you become the boss and achieve wild success, the mantras and advice tend to flow in abundance. Over time, with the benefit of hindsight and varied experiences, I have come to realise there's no single winning playbook, no universal culture mantra, no perfect hiring tip, no ultimate meeting strategy, or a one-size-fits-all template. The reality is that there are countless mantras, each shaped by different environments, unique contextual factors, cultural differences, and constraints that make a copy-paste approach ineffective.

Reflect on your own circumstances, draw inspiration, and adapt practices to suit your context. Blindly believing that what worked for someone else will work for you isn't the answer. Just my perspective.

So, as you navigate your leadership journey, remember to take advice with a grain of salt—or maybe the whole salt shaker—and tailor it to fit your style. After all, you are the one in the driver's seat. Just make sure you are not following someone else's GPS to the wrong destination. Happy steering!

EPILOGUE: WHAT TRULY MATTERS

*'The more you know who you are and what you want,
the less you let things upset you.'*
—**Bob Harris**, *Lost in Translation*

As you reach the end of this book, think of it not as a conclusion but as a beginning—a chance to carry forward the ideas, lessons, and moments of insight that resonated with you. The journey of growth and self-discovery doesn't end here; it continues in the choices you make, the perspectives you embrace, and the way you navigate the world.

To leave you with something meaningful, the book closes with two reflective pieces that serve as reminders of what truly matters.

What We Need Versus What We Get

The experiences we need are expensive.
The clothes we don't need are cheap.

The friends we need are far away. The acquaintances we don't need are on our screens.

The peace we need is elusive.
The noise we don't need is in our ears.

The politicians we need are absconding.
The scoundrels we don't need are incharge.

The connections we need are fading.
The connectivity we don't need is growing.

The path we need is waiting for us.
The race we don't need is the one we are running in.

Get Home Safely

Someone is waiting for you.
Your partner. Your kids. Your friends. Your parents. Your pet.

You matter.
To your families and the world around you. Much more than to any company.

Your company can do easily without you.
Your loved ones cannot.

You are important for your project.
You are irreplaceable to your family.

Your work pals are good for a drink.
Your family is good for life.

Do your best at work.
and then, most importantly,
Get home safely.

ENDNOTES

'Much to learn, you still have.'
—**Yoda**, *The Empire Strikes Back*

Here's a list of books and articles that have influenced me over the years. While I don't claim they are the best or recommend them outright, I have found them invaluable in helping me make sense of my work-life journey.

You Versus You

- Stephen R. Covey, *The 7 Habits of Highly Effective People*
- Jordan B. Peterson, *12 Rules for Life*
- Morgan Housel, *Same as Ever*

- Adam Grant, *Think Again*
- Adam Grant, *Hidden Potential*
- Dr Spencer Johnson, *Who Moved My Cheese?*
- Scott Galloway, *The Algebra of Happiness*
- Byron Sharp, *How Brands Grow*
- Daniel Pink, The Puzzle of Motivation (YouTube)
- Simon Sinek, Why Good Leaders Make You Feel Safe (YouTube)
- Simon Sinek, How Great Leaders Inspire Action (YouTube)
- Admiral William H. McRaven, Make Your Bed (YouTube)
- Daniel Levitin, *How to Stay Calm When You Know You Will Be Stressed* (TED Talk)
- Be Somebody, Stop Asking for Easy (YouTube)
- James O'Toole and Warren Bennis, *A Culture of Candor*
- Guy Winch, *How to Turn Off Work Thoughts During Your Free Time* (TED Talk)
- Gaur Gopal Das, *Life's Amazing Secrets*

You and Others
- James Surowiecki, *The Wisdom of Crowds*
- Will Guidara, *Unreasonable Hospitality*
- Simon Sinek, *Start with Why*
- Robert B. Cialdini, *Influence: The Psychology of Persuasion*
- Jeremy Heimans and Henry Timms, *New Power*
- Dan Ariely, *Predictably Irrational*
- Tom Wujec, *Build a Tower, Build a Team* (TED Talk)

Future You

- Eric Barker, *Barking Up the Wrong Tree*
- Charles Duhigg, *Supercommunicators*
- Sheena Iyengar, *The Art of Choosing*
- Héctor García and Francesc Miralles, *Ikigai: The Japanese Secret to a Long and Happy Life*
- John Kotter, *Our Iceberg is Melting*
- Shunmyo Masuno, *Don't Worry: 48 Lessons on Achieving Calm*
- Mikael Krogerus and Roman Tschäppeler, *The Decision Book*
- Hubert Joly, *The Heart of Business*
- Jim Collins, *Good to Great*
- Steven Bartlett, *The Diary of a CEO*
- Derek Sivers, How to Start a Movement (YouTube)
- Professor Clayton M. Christensen, *How Will You Measure Your Life?*
- Linda A. Hill and Kent Lineback, *In Pursuit of a Better Boss*
- J. Sterling Livingston, *Pygmalion in Management*
- Valorie Kondos Field, *Why Winning Doesn't Always Equal Success* (TED Talk)

ACKNOWLEDGEMENTS

'There are three ways to ultimate success:
The first way is to be kind. The second way is to be kind.
The third way is to be kind.'
— **Fred Rogers, *A Beautiful Day in the Neighborhood***

Writing a book is never a solo endeavour; it's a journey built on the shoulders of those who inspire, guide, and support you. This book is a culmination of countless lessons, encouragement, and love from the extraordinary people in my life.

I would like to express my gratitude to my late father, whose high expectations and approach to life continue to guide me.

I carry your lessons with me every day, and this book is as much yours as it is mine.

To Maa, who ensured I was brought up right and had everything I needed to succeed. Thank you for being the guiding force that quietly pushed me to be better.

To Ruchi, my better half and best friend. Thank you for your patience, love, and for keeping me grounded when I start to drift too far, and for kicking my butt when I get lazy! You have been my anchor and compass through it all.

To Ved and Neil, my bundles of joy and chaos. Thank you for teaching me more about life than I ever imagined. Your energy, questions, and laughter light up my days and remind me what truly matters.

To my teachers, from the kind soul who taught me to tie my shoelaces to the professors who opened my mind to new worlds. Their influence has been immeasurable. I am deeply grateful to my bosses for the lessons, challenges, and, yes, the occasional free lunch. You have all contributed to this journey in ways you may not even realise.

A special thank you to my persistent editor, Aditya Jarial, who refused to let me settle for 'good enough'. His insistence on sharpening every word and thought has made this book so much better, even if it tested my patience at times!

And to everyone who has helped along the way and been so generous with their time and advice. As Jerry Maguire famously said, 'You complete me.' This book wouldn't be what it is without the incredible support of my family, friends, and colleagues. I just happened to be the one holding the pen.

www.ingramcontent.com/pod-product-compliance
Lightning Source LLC
LaVergne TN
LVHW041701070526
838199LV00045B/1147